OVERSTANDING DARKNESS

Conscious-Elevation:
Keys to Developing Your Awareness

By

Michael Campbell

Cover Art by Marlin T Boga

authorHOUSE™

1663 LIBERTY DRIVE, SUITE 200
BLOOMINGTON, INDIANA 47403
(800) 839-8640
WWW.AUTHORHOUSE.COM

AuthorHouse™
1663 Liberty Drive, Suite 200
Bloomington, IN 47403
www.authorhouse.com
Phone: 1-800-839-8640

AuthorHouse™ UK Ltd.
500 Avebury Boulevard
Central Milton Keynes, MK9 2BE
www.authorhouse.co.uk
Phone: 08001974150

This book is a work of non-fiction. Unless otherwise noted, the author and the publisher make no explicit guarantees as to the accuracy of the information contained in this book and in some cases, names of people and places have been altered to protect their privacy.

© 2007 Michael Campbell. All rights reserved.

No part of this book may be reproduced, stored in a retrieval system, or transmitted by any means without the written permission of the author.

First published by AuthorHouse 3/20/2007

ISBN: 1-4208-6108-5 (sc)

Printed in the United States of America
Bloomington, Indiana

This book is printed on acid-free paper.

Forethought

What we basically have is a Conscious Scale of Development- Staring off first: Physical/chemical body

Strong influences on behavior- biological

Gross material: Physical/Bodily needs-

Food, Water, Shelter, Family, Science. . . . . . .

To (physical/emotional connection)

Emotional understanding and control: Emotional needs within the body and outside of the body/ Commitments or Royalty to self and to others deserved or underserved.

Dealing with negative emotions safely and honoring what's worth honoring.

(This is the start of responsibility and emotional control.)

To (social/emotional connection)

Social class/duty: Dealing with an Individual's actions and your own actions/ friendships/ social rank: *Social position, moral development and personal communications with peers, mature mind filled with love and knowledge is needed for this blended high energy thought. There is a power in Love that allows one to increase their mental capacity to learn. When one strives for continuous learning it causes the mind grow stronger and it unveils the mental world around use.*

To (social/emotional/mental-connection)
Mind: Coordinates five senses, physical, emotional and social events with inner thoughts and motives. The mind is the constant

unifier of millions of sensations, focused into the physical body that has needs of their own. Its powers are used for good and for bad depending on how is it trained:

You train your mind with your likes and dislikes. If you don't learn or are led to like positive things, things that open the mind, as compared to things that lock the mind into single trains of thought. *An Open Mind can See no End*. **The Ending of one journey or dimension starts the beginning of the next one. We are all Multi-dimensional Beings living under the Stress of being spiritual in a material minded world. That said:** *Every Thought has WIEGHT, SHAPE, SIZE, FORM, COLOR, QUALITY, and POWER. Although this mental energy is invisible to the eye, the mind feels and processes these thoughts. Some personalities are happy and spread good vibes to those around them, while some selfish personalities can drain you or make you feel uncomfortable. Unfortunately, many* **humans on earth project force-fields of hate**. *These thought's effect our Aura's, our Bodies of Light, that surround our physical body. Your aura can mix with others and even leaves a trail behind you where ever you may travel. Thoughts can even get caught in others thoughts causing another individual to think something or they can fade back into the Infinite Mind. This energy of thoughts is very small in material quantity, yet focused and concentrated its effects can by felt be others (telepathy).* **These are the fruits of the Spirit and gifts of the Spirit if you have tasted them**.

You can build mental fabric by finding 120 degrees of correct knowledge, 120 degrees of correct wisdom, and 120 degrees of correct understanding, about the world around you. When 360 degrees is reached our mental velocity starts its spin, as its spin increases, it creates an awareness of higher thought patterns. This type of thought can reach into the invisible world of the Mind sensing the Spirit. This contact causes an increase in mental velocity that broadens consciousness and deepens our Understanding of Self. It causes a **second and most times third break down in a person's mind, a kind of thought consolidation of all sciences known and understood, plus understanding of all you know about the world and universe.** *At this level of thought your core principles and* *science should merge to reveal the one science that all others come from. You develop a foundation that builds character and mental awareness. Your minds' churning process (ciphers) evolves/spins by keeping right knowledge, wisdom, understanding and getting rid of what's stopping progression. This process will continue throughout life so that all of your life is learning and adapting new sciences with old and new techniques. Thought becomes powerful as its form changes due to conscious effort, to build more Mental Power.*

But why is this important! It gives each of us purpose and a destiny to fulfill.

What is Destiny?   What is Purpose?
Living is not just about being alive but growing in conscious experience about your physical body with its **Emotional, Mental, and Spiritual Evolutions unfortunately all** *happening at the same time. As you can see, as with most of us, it's very difficult to understand and it therefore causes a lot of pain and suffering in the world. We are bombarded by millions of sensations and stimuli each day and we are trying to grow and grasp an ever changing body to control ourselves. But, Destiny is a conscious choice of the way one lives their life. It is living in a physical existence with spiritual laws that govern your actions. Only through the connection with destiny can the Revelations be fully understood on all levels of awareness. Having the willingness to follow with Mental Understanding of how higher Principles can affect the earth as well as open your Mind. We have an infinite ability to learn, to do, and to be. Physical Sciences are ten to hundreds of dominoes behind Spiritual Sciences in the way change occurs. Destiny will show the past as the future, and the future as the present and the present a channel to build what's good and destroy what's bad not only in you but around you. The real problem is that to get to this level of destiny, you must know about your true Self. Only through Knowledge of Self can one's Destiny or life, not just living, be fully understood. This brings an appreciation of the bad moments in an individual's life as well as the good.* <u>*You start to recognize that it is the* **Struggle** *in life that makes us strong and is necessary for us to grow and fulfill our destiny.*</u>

From a gross material body to the invisible workings of the mind and spirit is where consciousness is found. By being conscious of each level or degree of conscious experience, we build a foundation from which we can explore the inner working of ourselves. This knowledge of self leads to deeper thought and deeper levels of conscious experience as well as physical awareness.

One level of Knowledge of Self, is Self-Reflection on childhood experiences, problems faced and conquered, plus those that ended in defeat. All these were Building Blocks of Personality. Those plus the Hidden Attributes that the Spirit/Mind can bestow. By looking deeply, as a third party viewer into our actions, into past experiences, we confront Our Own Short Comings! We also continue to Grow and strengthen our Feeling of Self. It's our Feelings about Ourselves and Knowledge of the work you did to better your self, that empowers you to live of life with some control. Once we realize our Higher Self, Spirit becomes our guide through the physical existence. Only when we truly and honestly listen can we benefit from its wisdom. Overstanding Darkness is an understanding of the darkness that clouds the Mind. Fill it with light to see through the darkness and science of the greater universe can be known. It's selfishness that clouds our vision and determines important outcomes that shape destinies. You must discipline your Mind and the world will unfold its truest gifts before you! You are what you think. As you view yourself mentally you also see your thought patterns and can feel your emotional state. Purpose! Is the Key ingredient to Conscious Elevation.

The Breakdown:

The purpose of teaching this is to open people's mind to new Idea's and to invite you to share in the experience of the education of the soul. *I would like to start by saying that I proclaim **spiritual liberty, teach eternal truth, and foster living faith.** As your soul is advanced, you become more conscious of self.*

<u>Evolution-</u> **Is the advancement of Conscious Power in Overcoming Physical Limitations and All Conscious States that would inhibit the full expression of the Love of the Creator in all the Kingdoms of Intelligence.**

*The people that survive past this **form of Evolutionary Survival** will continually gather light and life into themselves. Light is in nature the source of all thought. Thought is energy. The light in the soul gets brighter as the soul evovles.*

Love leads Insight
Overstanding =Energy= Soul's Glow

Slow progressive of thought

Animal to Beast	Beast to Man (Homo-Erectus)
Man to Human (Spirit given in Melanin enhancement)	Human to Human Being (Spirit expands to energize thoughts)
Human Being to Being (Spirit project "The Infinite Way")	Being to Supreme Being (Spiritual clothes Infinite Mind)
Supreme Being to Supreme	And on and on

With added Love (Understanding) comes added Consciousness!
Highest

The Many Degree's LOVE

Love for ALL --------------Infinite Love---------------Righteous Love
Many Layers between -------------------------------------Degree High
Spiritual Love-----------Gifts of the Spirit
Infinite Layers between ----------------------------Transition Degree
Intellectual Love -------Love of Science and Knowledge
Family Love--------------Love of Family
Material Love-----------Love of Objects
Selfish Love -------------Love of Self---------------------- Degree Low

Lowest

The most important thing we must learn is about Love and the hidden value of loving children. A father's Love for a child can enhance awareness and built spiritual energy faster then anything else on earth. Through knowledge of self, raising children strengthens the bond between the Creator and the human mind. <u>This amazing contact leaves Fruits of the Spirit behind to help the mind function at a higher rate to meet the demand of raising children that are smarter and more determined than ever.</u> Children are the Creator's Tool's to test us and brings fourth blessings to parents or relatives. Universal Love of all things, especially humans, can bring our minds to a higher level of Cosmic Awareness and True Spiritual Liberty. A stagnate soul is a dying soul. Higher Intelligence sees evolution from the physical body as a deeper understanding of life as a Multi-Dimensional Being.

Multiple Dimensional Evolutions

Of the inner Worlds - STEADY PROGRESSION ON THE

PHYSICAL LEVEL (Physical change)

EMOTIONAL LEVEL (Emotional maturity)

MENTAL LEVEL (Mental mastery)

SPIRITUAL LEVEL (Spiritual awareness)

Social Levels are combination of all

Plus social pressure to succeed

CONTAINED IN HUMAN'S DAILY EVOLUTION

Descending Creations

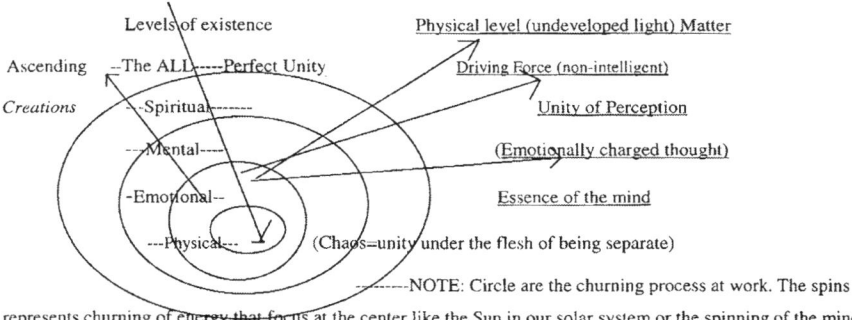

Levels of existence — Physical level (undeveloped light) Matter

Ascending — The ALL — Perfect Unity — Driving Force (non-intelligent)

Creations — Spiritual — Unity of Perception

— Mental — (Emotionally charged thought)

— Emotional — Essence of the mind

— Physical — (Chaos=unity under the flesh of being separate)

-----NOTE: Circle are the churning process at work. The spins represents churning of energy that focus at the center like the Sun in our solar system or the spinning of the mind that should grow stronger and larger as we live. The universe is expanding and contracting that the same time. Our sun spins on its axis also and at the center it is far hotter than on the surface. ***The churning process is growth in the universe and in the Human.***

<u>Descending Creation</u> - Perfectly created beings descend to create life in lower heavens in the Image of the Creator (Adams & Eves)

<u>Ascending Creations</u>- Imperfect creations ascending towards perfection (dimension by dimension)

To redeem ourselves means *actually to reprogram ourselves, not only for the benefit of the humans on this planet, but for spiritual liberation working with all vibrations from the kingdoms of Light within the Greater Universe.* ***Spiritual liberation*** *is to <u>go beyond the "Closed Structures" of religions in the world that ignore Pluralistic Kingdoms and the many Creators of Light in First Source and Centers</u>*

Eternal Family. These religions sanction *"**Authoritarianism**"* and *suppress the creative act of the **Holy Spirit**. We have to understand how the vibrations of our Conscious Time Zone connects with all those worlds previous to, parallel to, and those that come after our own Time Zone. Only then can we, as a transformed creation, truly redeem our race to become one with the **Brotherhood of Light** so we to can participate in the many realms of experience.* <u>***Each person is given a responsibility to exercise their "Will Power" to either destroy themselves in the darkness or accept, ever lasting life, the higher "law of Light " through faith and love.***</u> *Progressing spiritually means to open your awareness up more fully each day from second to second and day to day in life. **Religion is an individuals' self-conscious experience between the Creator and man through faith**. Progress means learning about the Father's Will and then trying to do the Fathers Will. That's how we raise our level of thinking to a new phase of **God consciousness***.

God Consciousness - Dual reality

Higher Self--Lower Self

<u>Divine Makeup</u>---Smokeless fire pure light	<u>Animal Makeup</u>---Matter-imperfect light
<u>True Consciousness</u>--No wants, no desires, no likes, no dislikes. Unity.	<u>Emotionally controlled consciousness</u>--Wants, desires, likes, dislikes, illusion of being a separate person from others
<u>Vibration</u> - High to infinite <u>Mind</u> – Infinite	<u>Vibration</u> - Low to very low <u>Mind</u> – Finite
<u>Power</u> – Omnipotent	<u>Power</u> – Limited
<u>Presence</u> - Omnipresent - dwells in all creations	<u>Presence</u> – Singular, separate entity
Highest Conscious expression - Creating the human expression on lower levels	Conscious Beginning - just above Man consciousness - to beast life - to organic matter

Elevation through creating in Creators image	Elevation through love and life and learning
Overstanding	Understanding

Higher Self and Low Self - Combine in the human experience
Humans being pulled in two directions

SPIRITUAL SIDE	ANIMAL SIDE
Sacrifice - Love	Wants – Needs
Patience - Insight	Desires – Satisfaction
Freedom	Control
Higher Self - represent as angels	Devil - represented as Lower Self

GOD CONSCIOUSNESS- is a dual reality with a physical base and a spiritual outlet. It's the consciousness of the workings of the inner you (mind and spirit and energies of the body) and the outer you (your environment). Mind must be aware of the presence/power of the unseen spiritual world and its effects on the seen physical world. *Being able to realize inner meaning, a kind of secondary breakdown of all knowledge one knows.*

Realization or Revelation?
1. An answer to a question that you didn't know how to ask.
    a. Happens unconsciously and is immediately perceived
    b. Answers vital questions needed for intellectual growth
    c. It tells you the question and answers it.
2. A builder of foundations to acquire growth in -
    1st. Right knowledge - to grow into right wisdom
    2nd. Right wisdom - to grow into right overstanding
    3rd. Right overstanding - to grow into an Infinite Mind
3. An unifier - it brings unity to one's abstract thought
    a. Adds unity to what's known
    b. Reason why some memories stay until understood

c. Unifies external stimuli from environment with internal sensations
    4. A mental strengthener
        a. Adds energy of overstanding
        b. Adds a secondary brake-down of knowledge
        c. Helps you to know that you have a true conscious choice in making decisions in life.
    5. A shower of destiny
        a. Reveals the inner worlds of Self Experience
        b. Shows Creators guiding hand of protection and control
        c. Shows your connection with the Creator
    6. Gives gifts from beyond your Physical Self

The ability to see beyond the lower manifestations of the physical are given only to the faithful witness of the Living Word of the Universal Father. To be a true citizen of our system you must have **Universal love, Cosmic Awareness, and deep spiritual insight** *or like a thief in the night, when in hard times, you'll resort back to your fleshly/animal ways.* <u>Facts can only take us so far where it ends, philosophy continues until it ends and then religion picks up and carries you to the further point it can, but faith, and faith only, can take you into the endless possibility of eternity and everlasting life.</u> *The religion of today are worldly and don't teach about the life's beginning before earth and the end after the earth, as you complete your souls training and from a follower of emotional self (lowest self) to a leader of Self (Mental Self) to a follower of your Divine Self (guided by the inner spirit). Find the Conscious Light on the inside in order to see and experience the truth, the only way is through individual experience. To stop progressing means to slowly fall back into your earthly/animal tendencies. Overstanding Darkness is about understanding your ego (lower self), your higher Self and different levels of consciousness and how the Father manifests his personality in each individual.*

Darkness and Blackness
Break down Part 2

Black is the back round for light to pass through and be seen. Black is what is seen when you close your eyes before the mental imagery starts flowing. Black is unity, without form, and the mixture of all colors blended in one. If you take all the colors and put them on top of each other, the color black appears. Black is the base element for things like tar, coal, oil. That's why the sky at night is black because the universe has all colors in it. Is color very important to human beings? Of course! The more melanin or blackness, (the Solid Form of Light) one has, the more one can absorb energy from the universe.

ETHER- THE MASTER MEDIUM
(Small gaps in space the light passes through - a black background)
Highest degree of Ether on the Physical Plane

FIRST ETHER	Medium of thought to thought, stored memories, brain transmissions, telepathy
SECOND ETHER	Medium for emotional waves, finer forms of electricity like heat and energy to muscles and nerves
THIRD ETHER	Medium for light, pranayama (energies from Sun)
FOURTH ETHER	Medium for electricity, heat, sound, magnetism

GASEOUS

LIQUID

SOLID

Lowest degree of ether on the Physical Plane (Melanin is a living form of ether)

That is, light and heat are the grosser (heavier) forms of purified energy. There is also subtler (lighter) energy of the universal proportion that gets absorb through the skin or in meditation through colors of the Chakras. You can get vitamin D directly from the sunlight and the energy you get from food can be directly placed in your major glands, in a purer form of light, through meditation. Melanin helps us stay in tune with the universal heartbeat and melanin gives rhythm in ways not understood by those with lesser of this divine agent. Even before the creation of the earth, Dark skin provided the best protection from exposure and disease.

Melanin is a type of Intermediary Ether in solid form needed for life. All animals and plants get their color from Melanin. Everything in nature has color because of Melanin. Darkness is the essence of the universe and melanin is its special solid light agent. Remember light evolved from Darkness.

Overstanding verses Understanding

Understanding can turn into Overstanding in time. Understanding is baby knowledge that we had when we were kids. Inner standing is knowledge in our adolescent stage of life. Now, Overstanding is the supreme consciousness, using maximum focused mind energy. You see, **first you need Right Knowledge** which is the foundation of all things in existence. **Then, you need Right Wisdom** which is the manifestation of our knowledge acquired. **Then you need Right Overstanding,** which is the most important, for it's the mental picture projected through ones knowledge and wisdom.

When you understand something you're basically standing under information as it drops down on you. To under-stand you have to grasp (catch) the information to become aware of how utilize it. Understanding sometimes is incomplete if you grasp only pieces of the information.

Overstanding Vs Understanding

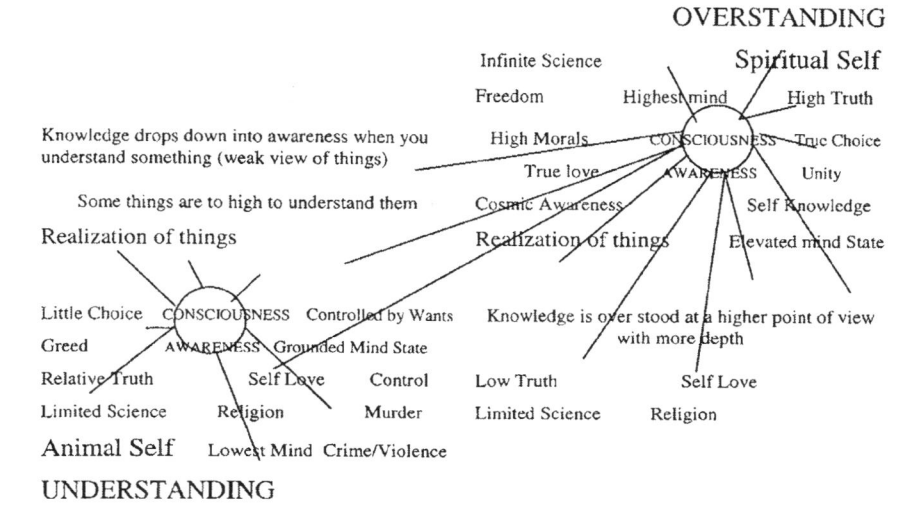

OVERSTANDING

```
                                    Infinite Science         Spiritual Self
                                    Freedom         Highest mind     High Truth
Knowledge drops down into awareness when you    High Morals──CONSCIOUSNESS──True Choice
understand something (weak view of things)           True love    AWARENESS    Unity
    Some things are to high to understand them   Cosmic Awareness      Self Knowledge
    Realization of things                        Realization of things  Elevated mind State


    Little Choice    CONSCIOUSNESS  Controlled by Wants   Knowledge is over stood at a higher point of view
    Greed         AWARENESS  Grounded Mind State                with more depth
    Relative Truth        Self Love      Control         Low Truth          Self Love
    Limited Science       Religion       Murder          Limited Science    Religion
    Animal Self    Lowest Mind  Crime/Violence
```

UNDERSTANDING

In overstanding something you are standing over the information looking down at it and therefore, experiencing the information from a higher point of awareness to truly know it. Information isn't necessarily knowledge because you have memorized it. First it has to be determined if the information is true or even relevant and does it connect or strengthen what you already know. **Knowledge can be checked by connecting with two of the three tests - Evidence, Experience, and Reason.** *When you understand you can miss some of the meaning because it falls down and dazes you or passes by. You can't make a caveman see the light without taking them through* **the process** *of a little light at a time (to reach full sight) or the light will dazzle him and he will still be blind.* <u>To overstand is taking understanding a step further to point of realization.</u>

I have done all the book work for you and now all you need on your path of enlightenment is effort. For those who really and truly want to progress, it is all here for you. For those who are curious, you will be surprised by the common sense that mixes with the knowledge so it's easily understood. I've given you more than one process and you can take them and use the one that suits your existing belief. The path of enlightenment is individualize, so for each person it will be slightly different but I've given you a few examples on how it works for me and the basic science on the internal working of the mind, spirit, and body. It will work for you too, maybe not the same way it did for me but all it takes is for you to give the right effort. **For with effort comes progress.** *It doesn't matter what religious background you have because my doctrine is all about love and overstanding the truth. The truth may be hard at first but if you accept it, it will forever be your friend. This book will cause you to look inside your self and find the divine nature that will make it possible for everlasting peace and harmony. For all life is about spiritual cultivation and growth.* Change is the one constant thing you can count on and change will change you sometimes negatively and sometimes positively depending on your spirit. *So, improve and change yourself by learning about Self.*

Thank the Creator for blessing me with the task of furthering the Divine Plan.

Overview: **The Highly Conscious Mind**

This book is a collection of the various prophets teaching about self discovery and a process of *elevation through thought*. There is a process for everything in life and if you want to achieve any goal than all you really need is a method of how to achieve your goal. As you might know big changes are on the horizon of the human race and as things like technology, philosophy, material comforts continue to grow and expand it becomes necessary for religions to grow with the changes or surely those same changes that enhance your life can cause its destruction. I have attempted to put together a way for each of you to feel and overstand what *Conscious Elevation* is all about. I want to show the **blend of spiritual/physical and religious/scientific theory** that will unite the all the doctrines of information to one cause. Our intellect is what separates us from our animal nature, our mentality, and our moral, and religious natures that especially distinguish us from the animal world. The selective response of an animal is limited to the motor level of behavior and usually appears only after trail and error. **Only personalities** can know what it is doing before it does it; **only personalities possess insight** in advance of experience. **A personality** can look before it leaps and can learn from looking as well as from leaping. When people fail to discriminate the ends of their mortal striving, they find themselves functioning on an animal level of existence. They fail to get the superior advantages of that material acumen (keenness), moral discrimination, and spiritual insight that are an integral part of our cosmic-mind endowment as an individual being.

The Thought Process
HIGH Degree of Thought-----More Love-More Insight and Awareness

Thought expands towards Spirit

Dimension 9-----thought expands on and on

Dimension 8---- thought expands to concern for all things on earth (plants, animal, people)

Dimension 7---- thought expands to concern for all people

Dimension 6---- thought expands to concern for all countries and most people

<u>Between Dimension are many levels that fade into one another</u>

Dimension 5---- thought expands to concern for ones own country and

Dimension 4--- thought expands to concerns for ones own state of affairs (New Yorkers)

Dimension 3---- thought expands to concern for society, neighborhood, surroundings

Dimension 2----thought expands to concerned for self, friends, family

Dimension 1---- thinks about one's own needs, wants, desire, selfishness

Thoughts contracts towards Material

LOW Degree of thought--------Less Love-Less Insight and Awareness

The supreme value of human life consists in the *growth of values*, *progress in meaning*, and *realization of the cosmic inter-relatedness* of all of these experiences. And **such an experience is the equivalent of God-consciousness**. Such a mortal, while not supernatural, is truly becoming superhuman; an immortal soul is evolving.

Doctrines from the Urantia Book:

Self-consciousness

Human self-consciousness is all about the recognition of the reality of our selves and others that are conscious of self. This further implies that such awareness is mutual; that self is known as it knows. Self-consciousness is in a communal consciousness: God and man, Father and son, Creator and created. In human self-consciousness four universal-reality realization are latent and inherent.
1. **The quest for knowledge, logic of science.**
2. **The quest for moral values, a sense of duty.**
3. **The quest for spiritual values, the religious experience.**
4. **The quest for personality values, the ability to recognize the reality of the Creator as a personality and the concurrent realization of our fraternal relationship with other (fellow) personalities. You become conscious of man as your created brother because you are already conscious of the Creator as your Creator Father.**

God-consciousness as it is experienced must consist of three varying factors or three differential levels of reality realization.
1st - *Mind Consciousness* **- comprehension of the idea of the Creator.**
2nd - *Soul Consciousness* **- the realization of the idea of the Creator.**

Last - *Spirit Consciousness* - is the realization of the spirit reality of the Creator.

By the unification of these factors of the divine realization, no matter how incomplete, the moral personality at all times overspreads all conscious levels with a realization of the personality of the Universal Father.

In the physical life the senses tell us of the existence of things; mind discovers the reality of meaning; but the spiritual experience reveals to the individual the true values of life. These high levels of human living are attained in the supreme love of "The All" and in the unselfish love of man. If you love your fellow men, you must have discovered their values. It is your thoughts, not your feelings that leads you God ward. The mind discerning right and wrong and possessing the capacity to worship Allah (the One), in union with a Divine Adjuster (Higher Self), is all that is required of a person to initiate and foster the production of his immortal soul of survival qualities. Only if such a spirit, that individually seeks the Father sincerely, desires to become like the Creator, and honestly elects to do the will of the Father in heaven.

The Creator's divine nature may be perceived only with the eyes of the mind. The mind's eye is what unifies your existence in the physical, mental, and spiritual activities. *<u>The Enlighten Spiritual Consciousness of a civilized man is not concerned so much with some specific intellectual belief or with any one particular mode of living. Their concern is with discovering the truth of living and the good and right technique of living and reacting to the ever-recurring situations of mortal existence</u>*. Moral consciousness is just a name applied to the human recognition and awareness of those ethical and emerging spiritual/physical values which duty demands that man shall abide by in the day-by-day control and guidance of conduct. Mind is a phenomenon connoting the presence-activity of living ministry in addition to varied energy systems; and this is true on all levels of intelligence. In personality, mind always intervenes between spirit and matter; therefore the <u>*universe is illumined by three kinds of light*</u>: ***material light, intellectual insight, and spirit luminosity.***

Universe is illumined by three kinds of light

LOWER LIGHT

Material light--------Physical Planes---Low vibration of light---Gives Illusions of us being separate entities---Material/Closed Minded---Mind corrupted/controlled by wants, needs, emotions, and others thoughts---Truth from belief ---Science Worldly---

Intellectual Insight--Mental Planes---From low material minds to Moral Thought--High vibrational degree-----Focused thought waves---Opening Mind---Truth from Faith and belief----Science Metaphysical and/or Religious

Spirit Luminosity---Spiritual Planes---Infinite degree of vibration---Infinite mental abilities (beyond human comprehension)---Angelic Worlds

HIGHEST LIGHT

Once your awareness grows to a certain level you will begin to overstand how the spirit and physical relate to each other and follow the moral values that come from that overstanding. Only as you cultivate morality and spirit does your conscious grow. Man cannot cause growth but he can supply favorable conditions for growth. Growth is always unconscious, be it physical, intellectual, or spiritual. Love thus grows; it cannot be created, manufactured, or purchased; it must grow, just as evolution is a cosmic technique of growth. <u>Man's sole contribution to growth is the mobilization of the total powers of his personality - living faith</u>. Living in truth and being faithful to that truth you know is not belief but living faith.

When the mind mobilization is focused totally on any level of psychic up reach towards spirit attainment, when there exists perfection of the human motivation of loyalties to the divine idea, and then there very often occurs a sudden down-grasp of the Indwelling Spirit. This causes a synchronization of the Infinite mind with the concentrated and sacred purpose of the super-conscious mind of the believing mortal. The more you help yourself, the more your indwelling spirit attaches comic energy to expand your mind (awareness) so you may receive a deeper comprehension of life. The mind of evolutionary man is confronted with the intricate problem of refereeing the contest between the natural expansion of emotional impulses and the moral growth of unselfish urges predicated on spiritual insight and a genuine religious reflection. The mind is unity; mortal consciousness lives on the mind level and perceives the universal realities through the eyes of the mind endowment. <u>Always must man's inner spirit depend for its expression and self-realization upon the mechanism and technique of the mind. Likewise must man's outer experience of material reality be based on the mind consciousness of the experiencing individual</u>. Therefore the spiritual and the material, the inner and outer, human experiences always correlate with the mind function and condition, as to their conscious realization, by the mind activity. Man experiences matter in his mind; he experiences spiritual reality in the soul but becomes conscious of this experience in his mind. The intellect is the harmonizer and the ever-present conditioner and qualifier of the sum total of mortal experience. Both energy-things and spiritual values are colored by their interpretation through the mind media of consciousness. The mind can and sometimes will portray to the human the experiential synthesis of energy, mind, and spirit in and as the Supreme Being. But the mind can never succeed in this unification of the diversity of reality unless such mind is firmly aware of material things, intellectual meaning, and spiritual values; only in the harmony of this trinity of functional reality is there unity, and only in unity is there the personality satisfaction of the realization of cosmic constancy and consistency. *The goal of human self-realization should be spiritual, not material. The mortal mind subservient to matter is destined to become increasingly material and will suffer eventual personality extinction meaning material decay. But, the mind yielding to the spirit is destined to become increasingly spiritual and ultimately achieves oneness with surviving and guiding divine spirit (Higher Self) and the mind will attain survival and eternity of personality existence (everlasting life). The only realities worth striving for are divine, spiritual, and eternal.*

There are three levels of universe reality and they are self evident to the clear reasoning and deep thinking minds. These levels are:
1. Causation - the reality domain of the physical senses, the scientific realms of logical uniformity, the differentiation of

the factual and the nonfactual, reflective conclusions based on cosmic responses. This is the mathematical form of the cosmic discrimination.
2. Duty - the reality domain of morals in the philosophic realm, the arena of reason, the recognition of relative right and wrong (based on culture, reason, evidence). This is the judicial form of the cosmic discrimination.
3. Worship - The spiritual domain of the reality of religious experience, the personal realization of divine fellowship, the recognition of spirit values, the assurance of eternal survival (everlasting life), the ascent from the status of servants of El (God) to the joy and liberty of the sons of The Most High. This is the highest insight of the cosmic mind, the reverential and worshipful form of the cosmic discrimination.

These are the three insights of the cosmic mind that constitute the necessary assumptions which make it possible for man to function as a rational and self-conscious personality in the realms of science, philosophy, and religion. Stated otherwise, the recognition of the reality of these three manifestations of the infinite is by a cosmic technique of self-revelation.

<u>Matter-energy</u> is recognized by the mathematical logic of the senses;
        ex. gravity

<u>Mind-reason</u> intuitively knows its moral duty;

<u>Spirit-faith</u> (worship) is the religion of the reality of the Spiritual

Experience.

These three basic factors in reflective thinking may be unified and coordinated in personality development and they produce a strong character that consist of correlations of a factual science, a moral philosophy, and a genuine religious experience. It's these three cosmic intuitions that give objective validity and reality to man's experience in and with things, meaning, and values.

It is the purpose of education to develop and sharpen these innate endowments of the human mind; of civilization to express them; of the life experience to realize them; of religion to ennoble them; and of personality to unify them. This is why through out this book I give you many different perspectives on the mind and consciousness. Only by recognizing and becoming familiar with the operations of the mind and consciousness can you change your thought process and open your awareness.

These qualities are the universal realities that are manifested in the human experience, on the following levels:
Body- It's the material or physical organism of man. It's the living electrochemical mechanism of animal nature and origin.

Mind and Higher Self- It's the thinking, perceiving, and feeling mechanism of the human organism. It's also the total conscious and unconscious experience. The intelligence associated with the emotional life reaching upward through worship and wisdom to the spirit level.

Spirit. The divine spirit that indwells the mind of man- Thought Adjuster (higher Self). The immortal spirit is pre-personal - not a personality, though destined to become a part of the personality of the surviving mortal creature.

Soul. The soul of man is an experiential acquirement and everyone does not have one functioning in him or her. As a mortal creature chooses to "do the will of the father in heaven," so the Indwelling Spirit becomes the father of a new reality in human experience. The mortal and material mind is the mother of this same emerging reality. The substance of this new reality is neither material nor spiritual it's morontial. This is the emerging and immortal soul that is destined to survive mortal death and begin the paradise ascension.

Personality. The personality of moral man is neither body, nor mind, nor spirit and neither is it the soul. Personality is the one changeless reality in an otherwise ever-changing creature experience; and it unifies all other associated factors of individuality. The personality is the unique bestowal that the Universal Father makes upon the living and associated energies of matter, mind, and spirit, and which survives with the survival of the soul.

Morontia is a term designating at vast levels intervening between the material and the spiritual. It may designate personal or impersonal realities, living or non-living energies.

The material mind is the arena in which human personalities live, our self-consciousness, and makes decisions to choose "Allah" or forsakes him, be a part of eternity or destroy themselves. The mind is a temporary intellect system loaned to human beings for use during a material lifetime, and as they use this mind, they are either accepting or rejecting the potential of eternal existence. Mind is about all you have of universe reality that is subject to your own will, and soul- the morontia self- will faithfully portray the harvest of the worldly decision that the mortal self is making. Human consciousness rests gently upon the electrochemical mechanism below and delicately touches the spirit-morontia energy system above. In neither of these two systems is the human being ever completely conscious of his life, therefore he must keep in mind that which he is conscious of. **And it is not so much what mind comprehends as what mind desires to comprehend that insures survival; it is not so much what mind is like as what mind is striving to be like that constitutes spirit identification.** It is not so much that man is conscious of the Creator as that man yearns for the Creator that results in universe ascension. What you are today is not so important as what you are becoming day by day and in eternity.

The mind is the cosmic instrument on which the human will can play the discords of destruction, or upon which this same human will can bring forth the exquisite melodies of spirit identification and resulting in eternal survival. The mind can actually be twisted, distorted, and rendered evil and ugly by the sinful machinations(plans, plots) of a perverse self seeking human. The mind also may be noble, beautiful, true, and good- actually great- in accordance with the spirit-illuminated will of a spirit-knowing human being.

Mind is your ship, your Divine Spirit is your pilot, and human will is captain. The master of the mortal vessel should have the wisdom to trust the divine pilot to guide the ascending soul into the morontia (spiritual/physical) harbors of eternal survival. Mind, in its essence, is functional unity; therefore mind never fails to manifest this constitutive unity, even when hampered and hindered by the unwise action and choices of a misguided emotional self.

Emotional Self
Contains the Animal Self and Beastly Nature

A. Emotional Thought:
   1. Influenced by
        a. Emotions
        b. Others stronger thoughts
        c. Environment
   2. Concentrates on
        a. Needs
        b. Wants
        c. Desires

B. Animal part - Human's bodily make-up (little control over instincts) is the number one cause of:
        1. Crime
        2. Murder
        3. Divorce
        4. Hate

C. Attitude Negatively Effects Body's:
        1. Nervous System
        2. Health and Sickness
        3. Digestion
        4. Organism and Cells
        5. Glands

This unity of mind invariably seeks for spirit cooperation on all levels of its association with selves of Will, dignity, and ascension prerogatives. During life the Human Will, the personality power of decision-choice, is resident in the material mind circuits; as terrestrial human growth proceeds the self, with its priceless power of choice, becomes increasingly identified with the emerging morontia-soul entity. When the human personality is completely identified with the morontia self and the soul is thus the embryo of the future vehicle of personality identity. <u>The soul partakes the qualities of both the human mind and the divine spirit but persistently evolves toward augmentation of spirit control and divine dominance through the fostering of a mind function whose meaning seeks to co-ordinate with true spirit value</u>. *If there is no survival of eternal values in the evolving soul of man, then mortal existence is without meaning, and life itself is a tragic illusion. But, it is forever true: What you begin in time you will assuredly finish in eternity- if it is worth finishing.*

CHAPTER I CONSCIOUSNESS
(Thought processing)

Let's start by saying that we are all conscious of our consciousness, conscious of our force and conscious of our form. In other words we know that we are alive, we know we have power (movement and thought), and we know we have bodies. What separates humans from animals is that animals are not conscious of being conscious and have limited motor skills. They know there is a means to a end but not if it's right or wrong in the way of achieving that end. Just like a plant will turn into the sunlight to get more sun or when you stick your hand in fire it will automatically jerk back. Human can override this reflect or instinct where animals can't. I'm not saying that animals have no intelligence because you can train them to learn different things like sign language for monkeys. But, there are limits to their intelligence were humans are unlimited in thier capacity to know and achieve. Animals only know their basic instincts and can not discriminate if it's right or wrong in the way they get to that end. This is why humans sometimes act like animals because they are following there low desires (animal craving), having no control over their actions. **If an animal is hungry it will eat anything according to its degree of hunger and some people demonstrate the need to satisfy their desires with the same nature.** *Some people can act civilize, while others don't, why? Well, there are different conscious levels in humans. Man has two natures within him; one is a low (animal self) nature and the other a high (divine Self) nature.*

The human beings don't have just one brain but three of them. *We have two animal brains and one civilizing brain to control the other two. The three brains are:*

1. **Brain Stem** (Reptilian Brain)- The oldest and most primitive part of the brain that exerts strong influence on our behavior. Controls the most primitive form of communication that is body language and gestures. That's how reptiles communicate. The brain stem controls your ability to experience and convey certain emotional states non-verbally like sadness, happiness and anger

by using facial or hand gestures. Body gestures are the way emotions manifest themselves in our awareness non-verbally. Behavior is also influenced by graphic symbols like printing, writing, and drawing on two-dimensional surfaces like a piece of paper. The Brain Stem is located at your spinal column that runs from your neck down to the lower back. It can also be seen in the reptiles back going down into their tail, thus called the reptilian brain and it's the seat of desires and your ego or lower self.

2. **Mid Brain** (Limbic or Mammal Brain)- This is the mammal brain that works through the brain stem. It is the seat of emotional communication that manifests it self in our awareness. Especially those emotional drives for fighting, fleeing, mating, and seeking food. The Mid Brain is located at the top region of the vertebrate right where the brain stem ends. The Mid Brain manifests itself through the Brain Stem when emotions are conveyed non-verbally. It's called the Mammal Brain because this is the brain of whales and other mammals that communicated emotionally (like humans). It's the seat of emotions in humans.

3. **Cerebrum** - Is the intellectual faculties and the civilizing function of the two animal brains (Brain Stem and Mid Brain). It's where mental activities are concentrated. The two hemispheres are the most dominant modes of perceiving and thinking about the world and the inner you. It is located at the top of the head above the Midbrain and it's the seat of divine power in man.

As you can see the human being has all the animals' brain in us, plus a special higher brain, which can use higher forms of energy. All your brains work together but the cerebrum can control the brain stem and midbrain once you have activated its higher faculties. **Activating the cerebrum's higher faculties is called Spiritual Cultivation.** *One must put more energy into it to trigger this activation. That's why some people are so emotional and others are not because the ones who aren't emotional have learned to control there animal brain (or suppress its affects) and therefore can turn* *there effects on and off almost at will. The stronger the emotion the harder it is to control but if you work on it you will see that it can be done no matter how strong the emotion may seem.* **Remember effort leads to progress**. *Not controlling ones passions and desires, following ones emotions blindly, is the number one problem in society today and selfishness is the reason for the high crime rate and low conscious energy level that most people operate on.*

PART 2   THE THREE FUNDAMENTAL STATES OF CONSCIOUS
(THE THREE ENERGY STATES) From The Metu Neter

Each Conscious State fades into the next one (many layers Between them)

Tamasic	Rajasic	Satvic
Understanding	Inner-standing	Overstanding
Mindfulness of wants, desires, copies, repeats	Self-consciousness or Self-awareness of emotions and attitudes	Mind's Eye or Third eye or Spiritual Eye, Aware of internal impressions
Physical sensation and senses	Inner Sight and Sensations	Clear Sight
Learns through knowledge and understanding of others	Learns through the accumulation of knowledge wisdom and understanding	Learns through Right knowledge, Right Wisdom, Right Overstanding plus Realization of truth
Limited Conscience effect	Conscience Vs Wants and Emotions	Motivated by Love and Truth

Follows Wants and Desires	Follows own Will	Follows Higher Selves Lead
		Deep Spiritual Insight and Cosmic Awareness

1. *(Understanding - Mindfulness)* **Tamasic** - Is the dream like or sleep like state of consciousness that is controlled by passions and emotions. In this state "Will Power" is very weak and cannot help but follow ones desires. This is what the Egyptian call **Mortals.** Mortals are those who have not yet attained the inner vision. They have an inner-voice or whisper that enforces desires no matter how good or bad they are. They have an animal mind because the "Will" is weak thinking is very limited pass the emotional level. This state of conscious requires very little energy because emotions provide all that is needed. It is a low energy state of consciousness and these people have weak soul (dim light) because they know not between right and wrong. They know they have wants and they live to satisfy them at any cost.

2. *(Inner standing - Self consciousness)* **Rajasic** - Is an awaken state of consciousness were the individual can go either to great accomplishment or struggle trying to do what's right. The individual starts to sense a kind of presence in their mind and this presence is the Light of Consciousness starting to evolve. They receive an inner voice or conscience and an inner-vision or mental projection. In this state "Will Power" is at normal levels and can contain the movement of some desires and emotions that don't feel right. One will fight with the thoughts of right and wrong either to conquer his desires and develop self-discipline or feel the pain of their conscience for their failure. This is the beginning of ones souls birth. This is what the Egyptians called **Intelligence's**. Intelligence's are those who had attained the inner vision or received the Light Conscious of the mind. At this level of consciousness the energy input has increase and will

continue to expand ones awareness as long as one is striving to make the right decision and put their emotions and wants under their "Wills" control. **THOUGHT + WILL (emotion or self forced) = ACTIONS**

3. (Overstanding- Mind's Eye) **Satvic** - Is a balanced state of energy that enables the full working of the highest state of spirituality. In this state one has full control over emotions and passions. One can then use the three most needed perceptions that are inner voice, inner sight, and inner overstanding. Earthy influences will vanish and thoughts can dwell in the spiritual realm. In this state the "Will Power" is at its highest level because it is mixed with the spirit and follows the Will of the Father. This causes the mind to be spiritualized and open its awareness to grow into God-Consciousness. It is in the conscious development and purification that separates the Eloheem (God body) from Man and not time and space. This is what the Egyptians called **creators.** Creators are those who have become identified with or united with the Light of the Conscious Mind. The Light being the truth of all things and brings Universal Love, Cosmic Awareness, and deep Spiritual Insight. The bonding with the soul's glow of higher righteous energy and eternal truth.

You see this is why some people act so strangely because they react to what they feel instead of using their minds to control their actions. They are slaves to their emotions with no "Will Power" to control their actions. When you are born you use more of your brain stem and mid brain because your cerebrum is still developing. <u>Your cerebrum needs input from its environment to process, without this input children would not develop properly (especially intellectually)</u>. Besides the cerebrum's ability of perceiving one must also cultivate its thinking ability to distinguish between right and wrong and get inner - overstanding which is the highest form of Knowledge of Self.

Our children are being educated incorrectly. As they grow to adult, like the adults of today, they'll have no control over their desires and society will continue to suffer from the ills that plague her. Crime and murder infest the world like bacteria, constantly multiplying. The element in question that has not been properly considered is education, not of the intellect but moral nature as I have stated which consist of the information of character and habits. **For education is the totality of the habits acquired**. *In other words, it is not just what the teacher teaches that the children remember but all their habits (good and bad) that teacher has. When the art of education is properly over stood (as to understood) and valued by each person, it will bring into the sphere of daily habits, forethought for one's self and those dependent on them, and respecting what is worthy of being respected. These habits will enable us to traverse (cross) periods of difficulty without being emotionally controlled with greater ease. The disorder and neglect in society are social sores that can only be cured by education rightly over stood.*

Now, lets get back to the three energy (or conscious) states. They are called energy states because each elevation causes for more energy to be used to maintain its condition. The three different states are awareness stages, at which people are conscious or unconscious of. The division from one conscious state to the next is hard to establish because it is difficult to tell where one ends and the other begins. There are many (infinite) levels in-between that lead up to full manifestation of one state to the other. In other words, if you draw two lines parallel to each other you will always be able to draw a line in-between them by using smaller and smaller tools to draw them. Therefore, you can only use the three fundamental states of consciousness (energy) as a guide.

Tamasic Consciousness Level (Mental Output)

<u>Energy level</u> - Low
<u>Engages in excess</u> - Eating, Drinking, Drugs, Sweets
<u>Inner Light</u> - None
<u>View</u> - Fragmented and Low
<u>Love</u> - of material things and satisfying emotional urges
<u>Learn through</u> - Definition, names, experience
<u>Self Control</u> - Little
<u>Sight</u> - External
<u>Senses focus on</u> - External objects

The **first state is the Tamasic** state *where people do what makes them feel good and follow there desires, with little restraint, no matter how cruel or evil they may be. All that matters to them is that they want it. They believe gossip and watch television, news, and follow the god of the dollar, being very materialistic. They follow the dollar because it will satisfy most of their greedy tendencies but their wants are never fully fulfilled because they always want more. They learn through names and definitions and verbal symbols to represent reality but to truly know one must insperience (not experience) it for themselves (not just memorize data). They learn by making distinction between things, based on their external differences. They seize upon the surface of things and separate the parts from the whole and members of a group from each other. In their consciousness there is too much distinction is being made between parts of a whole and members of a group. You see, verbal language and thinking function are incapable and cannot express realties of higher spiritual realms, especially those of the subjective realm where reality is formless (formless things can not be described in verbal language). When you look into the vastness of your mind you are looking into the subjective realm or your own mini universe.*

Objective Realm	Subjective Realm
Trying to Achieve Harmony	Perfect Harmony
Realm of Objects	Formless Reality
Division of the Whole	Perfect Unity
Many Things	No things (or One Thing)
Understanding	Overstanding
High to Low Planes	Highest Planes
Light and Darkness	Perfect Light or Darkness

What has no form cannot be named, described, or defined. We live physically in the Objective Realm where things have form. The subjective realm is living and the objective realm (lower realm) is doing. The subjective is life or just being, there is no death. Everything is in unity because they're no objects (meaning no formed things) in the highest realms. The only way to access these higher planes is to insperience (experience on the inside) through pure conscious. There is no individualism in the subjective realm. Activities in the highest realms of being cannot be referred to as "experience" as the term is prefixed with the sign of external events, "ex". To " insperience" something is on the inside and not the out. Inside of our mind and body, only you can know what is going on because words can't describe the indescribable sensations. The people at the Tamasic level of consciousness segregate everything, and this is why we have so much discrimination in the world today. Always segregating people by state, nation, color, race, gender, and etc. They are unable to see the harmony in nature and in people as one whole organism on one planet together. The nature of their faculty to separate is opposed to the very essence of the **hu***man being, which is Unitarian (to unite). They separate things into words and definition thinking that they know exactly what their describing. True knowledge is insperience, so what they know is other people's opinion. These reason and others is why the Egyptians called them* **"mortals"** *because they had to instructed them on how to learn and receive Knowledge of Self. These are just some of the characteristic that describes the Tamasic state of consciousness.*

Rajasic Consciousness Level (Mental Output)

Energy level - Medium
Engages in excess - Struggles against right and wrong
Inner Light - Yes
View - Part holistic / Part partial
Love - Differs depending on choice most of time
Learn through - Definition, experience, picture, some inner-experience
Self Control - Part Emotion/ part Will Power
Sight - External/ Limited Internal
Senses focus on - Environment, Emotions, Thoughts

Next, **in the Rajasic state** *the individuals begin to think for themselves. They start to see their actios and thought for what they are. Their conscience becomes strong and louder than the whisper it was in the Tamasic state. The Egyptians called these people "**intelligence's**" because now they have attained the inner vision or the Light (energy) of a mind. This energy is the power of thought, to be able to unite meaning and categorize information to further insperience it, (by relating it to personal experiences) for realizing how each thing is <u>one thing</u>. The <u>one thing</u> is everything that you know combined together working in harmony. Any information after this point has to be excepted into the one thing (all the knowledge you've acquired) to get any overstanding of it, if not it falls out of your range of comprehension unless you study or research it.* **Man's "Will" is free, no longer controlled by emotion, but now starts to follow divine law**. *They are able to ignore emotional and over ride the basic instincts as the divine parts of self start to grow. In this state of energy (consciousness) one can see that there are internal differences, as they increase their energy input, the inner factors strengthen and unify things based on the mutual relationship and interdependence of a thing with each other and the whole (start to take a holistic view).*

Knowing Vs Thinking

Automatic	Searching Memory (use of Will)
What's already Known	Inner Conversation - Thoughts - verbalizing what's known
Higher Self – Omniscience	Low Self wants to communicate what's known
Feeling - Everything known at once (intuition)	A process of retrieving information bits
Whole Story that brakes down	Partial story - bits and pieces
Unproduced reaction – known	Produced reaction

Knowing proceeds (comes before) thinking and its independence of thinking can be seen by any one who takes time to carefully observe their thinking process. **Thoughts are a sort of inner conversation "with one's self"(Inner standing/ consciousness). In reality, it is the process by which what is already known, (without words) is given verbal form**. *A very instructive exercise is to cut off the statements before the mental sentences are complete. It will be clear that you didn't need to complete the mental verbalization to know what was going to be thought. The problem with definitions, however correct or useful, is that their possession does not constitute knowledge. For the spiritual ones, that can feel, know that feeling comes before thinking and is completed in a faction of a second.*

At the Rajasic level of conscious energy from the cerebrum is in constant motion in controlling the lower brains (brain stem and midbrain) so that all of them can work together in unison. The Creator made us in its own image, not in physical characteristics, but in intellectual ability to know and to do as we access our higher abilities. This is how the Creator saves his children by letting them share in the omniscience (all knowing) part of its self. Not in the same magnitude or quantity as the Creator because we have to work through time, space and the Creator does not. In smaller attributes we have limited access to the knowing at this conscious level. That is why you already know what you're thinking before you mentally verbalize the information in your thoughts. All the information is inside of you but it is very difficult or at least takes a lot of energy to change the knowledge into verbal form. That's why mortals (Tamasic state) cannot access it because they don't have enough energy (Light of Mind) and why the intelligence's only have partial use of it. The further within we (insperience) withdraw our consciousness, the more energy it takes and the more we learn about our selves (knowledge of self). Knowing and thinking are two entirely different processes. Where as the mortal can only see how separate we are on the outside of self, the intelligence's (as the Egyptians called them) could start to see, not only on the outside but on the inside too, in a harmonious way. They have more of the total picture, therefore, more consciousness then the mortal that sees in one direction and not in multiple directions. Consciousness falls between the three levels in infinite forms because it takes time, as one strengthens the mind, to bring it self into full manifestation on one level. *When their working on this level and have reached full (or almost full) use of it's faculties they automatically start to progress to the next. Your higher energies are always there, just in latent (undeveloped) potential, but we can all raise our levels through this process of spiritual cultivation.*

Satvic Consciousness Level (Mental Output)

<u>Energy level</u> - high (very creative)
<u>Inner Light</u> - Identifies with inner Light
<u>View</u> - Holistic and Elevated
<u>Love</u> - of Spiritual things High and Low
<u>Learn through</u> - Insperience and Experience, intuition
<u>Self Control</u> - high and follows Conscience and Higher Self
<u>Sight</u> - Inner and Outer
<u>Senses focus on</u> - External objects and internal impression

Finally, the **Satvic state** *is the highest state of spirituality, when one has raised his level of awareness to that of God Consciousness. In this state you have a balance amount of energy in your being to open the door to spiritual perfection and inner peace. You will be freed from all materialistic wants and desires. You will die to physical things of this world and place yourself beyond the control of earthly sensations. Your new aim is to love and help others to progress and elevate their consciousness to its highest level also (share the Light of the Mind). In the bible it says that, "man is made in the likeness of the Eloheem", this means that the Creator's traits of Omnipotence (all power), Omnipresence (everywhere at once), and Omniscience (all knowing) reside in man as his or her essential qualities. Man's unlimited potential is subject to manifest itself through time and space (through the order or laws of the universe), while Allah's potential is not (manifests instantly). What the Creator can do in an instant, man can do also if given enough time (lives) and the right conditions (space). Its bases is on the fact that the Creator has actually incorporated itself and it's attributes into man's spirit, constituting man's self and his or her true faculties (higher nature).* **Yahweh saves man by endowing humans with its three divine attributes of all knowing, all powerful, and all present.**

The true worship, the true honoring, the true love and praising of Allah is in the striving to be God-like in action and in thought and to awaken the divine qualities that are the essence of our being. The Egyptians called this state of consciousness ***"creators or Son of the Light"****. The creators were identified with or united with the Light of the Mind and this automatically inspired you to do good acts as a form a creating, where as, doing an evil act is a form of destroying. The Conscious Light being, at this level is using their energy for creating. At this stage you have full use of our omniscience (Ability to learn what one needs to know from within theirspirit) that is true wisdom. When one has fully awakened at this level you will know that our true manifested self is the unity of all living being in the world. We should know through direct insperience that there is, only one dwelling intelligence in reality, in infinitude of living things in the world. In other words the same being that makes me and you conscious (in our individualized personality) is the same in all human being. We all share in a portion of the Universal Conscious Mind because consciousness cannot be divided or separated but bestowed upon us all. The difference in attitude and styles is the knowledge that comes from the different experiences that each individual has lived and gone through. You are all that you experience and think you are.*

Human Composition and the Energy States

The human composition is make-up of four separate parts that all work in harmony with each other. Of the four parts only one part is conscious of its consciousness, while the other add to the conscious experience by giving sensations and organization to it. The four parts of our human composition are Self, the Mind, the Energy System, and the body. The only one with consciousness is the Self, while the others contribute to its experience.

1. **Self**- Is the consciousness in each of us that we share with the Creator. It "Wills" and initiates activities and is the only part of the human that is conscious. Careful study would reveal that it is self and not the faculty involved in thought process, the mind that Self works with, that has the property of overstanding and knowing. Self is also that which feels and wills because knowing and feeling

are all modes of perception. **The Self perceives thought generated by the mind, the feelings (sensation) by the body, and events in the environment.**

1. **SELF**
A. <u>Passive mode</u> - In this mode self is that part that knows and feels in all modes of your perception.
B. <u>Active mode</u> - In this mode self Wills activities in the mental and Wills activities in the body. (Thoughts and physical movements)

2. **Mind**

Is that which processes thought, like a traffic guard controls the flow of traffic, the mind controls how fast or slow thoughts come-in. It cannot stop the flow of thoughts but can only speed them up or slow them down or focus them on one thing. Try to stop your thought consciously and you will see that you can't but you can slow them down to almost a stand still through meditation. Most psychologists say that the mind is conscious but if it were you wouldn't be conscious of your mind movements. You know when your mind is confused (thoughts moving to fast), or peaceful (thoughts slow), or relaxed and you would not know this if your mind were conscious. If you concentrate quietly you sense thoughts coming and going and the part that is feeling and overstanding of those thoughts are separate from them. (**Self**)

3. **Energy System**

Is the driving force for the physical, mental, sensory (pain, pleasure, perception) and emotional (psychic, attraction and repulsion) activities. This driving force is a blind force and the same force that controls the Tamasic (Mortals) state of consciousness. When I say blind force I'm saying that there's no intellectual factor in them that is concerned with right or wrong. That is why they cause so much damage when not properly used and controlled. An overstanding of this energy system is a must to bring about self-discipline and it leads to knowledge of self.

4. **Physical body**

Enable us to act on and in the physical plane. It is also gives us the illusion of being separate entities but the Self in me that's conscious and in you is the same because we all share a small piece of the Universal Mind that linked us all together in consciousness. The body is also the seat of your desires and wants where the energy system manifests its force through and in most people undetected.

In the Satvic state you are in constant contact with your Indwelling Intelligence (Higher Self) which has knowledge of the working of the universe can be relayed to you in meditation, deep concentration or even while you sleep. You'll find your true and only purpose of being on earth is the resurrection of the indwelling intelligence, so that it can guide your endeavors in life with the same omniscience that is uses to guide your physiological and subconscious mental activities. (Ex. cellular repair, digestion, blood flow, growth, etc...) Once you can identify about what level of conscious you are at, you can begin to take steps to elevate it to the next level. You won't really realize your true state until you pass through one between states to the next.

Along with the three levels of consciousness comes the way that they receive and interrupt information. These three modes of mental operations are important because one cannot arrive at the truth unless the process which one follows, in getting knowledge, is correct. The three modes of mental operation are syllogistic logic, synthesis, and wisdom. At each state of conscious there is a mental operation that goes with it.

Syllogistic Logic - Learns Through
Induction - deduction - Inference
Use of symbols and definition - that represent what reality really is or could be
Low Knowledge - based off other opinions

In the Tamasic level of consciousness the individual would use syllogistic logic. *Syllogistic logic is the arrival at a conclusion through induction, deduction, and inference. The logical thinking* *is done through symbols that are definitions that stand for what is really to be defined and explained. Just because one hears or knows a definition (symbols) for something in reality, doesn't mean that they know what the reality is truly. They confuse knowledge of definitions with the knowledge of the realties defined. Victimization by definitions is not limited to abstruse (complex) spiritual subjects but it applies to every area of the non-mechanical study like Psychology, History, Economics, Money, and etc. This is where the western medicine falls into trouble with their incorrect definition for illness and disease, remedies and cures. <u>Illness is in the mind and disease is in the body</u>. When you drink to much alcohol at first it is only your mind that is affected because it shoots off your perception (slow speech, put you off balance) that is the illness. The next day the disease comes in with the vomiting and a headache. Even though your perception have return too normal, the illness is gone but the disease that affects the body is not. In a similar manner things classified as poisons can be medicine and medicines can be poisons it all depends on the amount given. If you give someone an overdose of medicine it could kill him or her, but the same things that are poisonous can be medicine in the right amounts. This is just an example of how definition can cause much confusion when believed as true.*

Synthesis - Learns through
Manipulation of symbols
Using abstract categories
Uniting of information
A second brake-down of meaning
Some insight behind the nature of things

At the Rajasic level of consciousness synthesis is used to arrive at a judgment through the manipulation of symbols (definition) embodying abstract analogies (comparisons*). In other words, one would take things that seem dissimilar, but are alike in some respects (ways), and group them accordingly because if they're similar in some ways they could be a abstract (special) grouping of how they are similar in other ways. Take for instance* *in eastern medicine, poisons can be cures and medicines can be poisons, it all depends on the dosage that is given. If one had an illness in the arm and another in the leg (that was the same problem just in different locations) they would be treated the same in eastern medicine. In western medicine they would treat them like entirely different because of their different location. Even though there were the same symptoms in different areas in the body they should be treated the same not different because it's the same problem. This will also show that a highly skilled position, as a doctor and not a very good one, can be in a low energy state like the Tamasic level of conscious. At the Rajasic level where energy is more focused and things like this becomes clearer.*

Wisdom - Learning through
Direct perception of reality
Use of intuition and insight
Overstanding of Self
Full insight behind the nature of things

In the Satvic level of consciousness the arrival at a conclusion or judgment is arrived at without going through the thinking process, that is, direct perception of reality it self, *without manipulation of symbols (definitions) that represent reality but through direct perception of reality itself. The ability to intuit (have insight on) the worldly and the spatial (without space) placement of things is called wisdom. One has full use of there omniscience part of there being and is able to intuit almost anything that one needs to know. It helps for one to perceive the relationship between all things, and to relate them to the whole. This requires a lot of energy to access this part of your being that can only be done in a trance or meditation state. This is why the intake and out take of energy (air) is so important because the higher level of energy one can intake is a directly proportioned to the state of consciousness one is functioning on.*

Energy = consciousness

CHAPTER II
FROM HUMAN BEING TO SUPREME BEING - CULTIVATION OF THE SOUL

What is true and real knowledge? **With knowledge there are two paths that one can take**. *The first path leads to the knowledge of the truth and the second is secondary because it leads to knowledge of other people's opinions. True knowledge is that which "being is" and not knowledge that is "not being" (or not active). The truth is "being," meaning unproduced and unchangeable. It is constant and always the same, so when your knowledge changes or doesn't hold up to this requirement it is not true knowledge. The only way to live forever is to spread the truth because it never changes. While you spread the truth, people will always remember it now and later on in generations to come. As long as you live and spread the truth your doctrine will be eternal (like the Creator) and your name will always be paired with it. Self knowledge or knowledge of self is the basis of true knowledge.*

Source of knowledge

True knowledge	Relative knowledge
Spiritual make-up/ Requires Right Reason	Material make-up/ Requires Little Reason
Belongs to Higher Self	Low Self
Active	Inactive
Unifies	Is bits and pieces
Unchangeable (known only in degree)	Changeable (due to relation)
Inner Realization	Basic understanding
Eternal	Mortal
To make a Choice one must 'Know'	

Michael Campbell

WISDOM SYNTHESIS SYLLOGISTIC LOGIC

The theory of knowledge states that true knowledge is in the perception of the underlying unity of the various opposites that make up the universe. *If information doesn't fit in with or bring together previous knowledge known, then it is just information, and won't turn into knowledge. If information you receive, that you think is knowledge, is outside your scope of understanding it does nothing for you. Right knowledge identifies with the individuals learning and what the individual has learned in some way, shape, or form. Wrong information gets remember but has no relevant meaning to it, that's why real knowledge teaches you something about yourself that's always remembered.* **Knowledge can be checked out by 2 agreeing with at least of the 3 tests-Experience, Evidence, and Reason.** *Our education system teaches a lot of information that gets remembered but really has no meaning to the individual's learning it, if one cannot relate to it. The Egyptian's had four doctrines, and many others, that they use to teach in their University long ago. The Egyptian's University would teach there students for forty years because when they graduated from the Egyptian's University, they would know all the universal sciences, and that's what University (universal knowledge) stood for. Back then all the people in the world would travel to Egypt to learn the working of the world like they do here in America. Most of the knowledge that we use today derived from the Egyptian schools in one way or another. The four doctrines that I am going to discuss from the Egyptian schools are the* **Transmigration of the Soul**, **The Law of the Opposites**, **The Summon Bonum or Supreme Good**, *and* **The Process of Purification**.

The Transmigration of the soul *doctrine has to do with the immortality of the soul and its salvation. True life is not found on earth, within time and space that is a testing ground for the spirit. The body is the tomb of the soul and it causes contamination (taking the high soul and putting it within the low body) by the soul's imprisonment in the body. Salvation is freedom of the soul from the body can only be achieved under purification or when its probation is complete. In other words your soul is trapped in your body and can only work through your body organs and glands to express itself.*

The body dampens the soul faculties and it can't express freely all of it attributes (Creator-like abilities). The difference in races of people is that spirit's expression's either helped or hurt by the type of body one has. The better the body, the better the expression of the spirit. You must be incarnated or born again into the flesh until you have purified your soul. Like it says in the scriptures," It would have been better for them not to be born, just too waste life on selfish desires". Being liberated from the chains of the flesh, a righteous soul acquires is pristine (pure) perfection, and joins the company of the Eloheems.

The Union of the Opposites *is the harmony in the union of the opposites like Yin and Yan, male and female, body and soul. As we look at even and odd we see the pattern that the opposites take. Even is being unlimited divisibility and odd being limited divisibility.*

Everything in our (conscious time zone) galaxy works off the law of the opposites. The Creator is everything and the Creator is no things. I know you are saying how can this be, but the reason is that, the Creator had to make a state of no things (triple stage of darkness) so that something can be born (99 attributes or elements plus the Creators name to make light). If the Creator is everything then Allah (the one) had to make a state of being that can live outside (yet still inside) of his all powerful essence, for us to have "free will" and not be subject to the Father's perfect will. Sensation is produced by the stimulation of the opposites like you sense cold because of the lack of heat. You would say that something is hard

because you know what soft is. If you are a hyper individual (high energy output) then you'll be a little cooler in the heat and a little colder in the cold because the higher level of activity you create has it effect in a opposite condition.

The Summon Bonum or Supreme Good *in man is to be God-like. Summon Bonum is the process of attainment, or transformation that is the harmony resulting from a life of virtue. It consists in a harmonious relationship between your lower nature (bodily wants, passion, pleasures) becomes controlled by ones higher nature (divine essence from the Creator) through the man to God application. The word "god" in ancient times meant " all being who appear to stand outside of the pale of ordinary humanity". Living a life of virtue means elevating from one to ten in the ten principle virtues and using your "Will Power" to change towards Allah's ways and thinking. Salvation is known as the development of the spirit from the animal stage to the human stage, the civilizing nature and developing a soul, to the spiritual stage, finding and following your Higher Self, which is being like El. <u>According to this principle, man is excepted to work out his or her own salvation</u>, <u>without a meditator between themselves and the Father</u>. This means the Creator is in Self and that if you looking for the Creator you'll only find him in inside of Self. There is no person that is between you and the Creator unless you put someone there. The Creator being on the inside of you as your pure consciousness seeing and knowing all you have done. It is true when they say that the Father feels the sorrows you feel and the joys also, because the Father is a living part of you. When Yashu'a (Jesus) said that," I am the Light and you must ascend to my father through me", he was referring to the Light inside self (the Spirit of Truth). This Light, is, the Light of the Mind and the Light of the Truth. All who don't see the Light must elevate themselves spiritually to see what the Light is (Conscious Light), which Yashu'a (Jesus) represented. One must first go through Light, which Yashu'a is apart of, to get to your divine nature, and once you bonded with the Light then you too will be apart of that same Light. We all have to go through and be touched by the Living Light to reach the Creator. This is what was meant by Yashu'a causing the blind to see the Light* *and the deaf to hear the truth and the lame to walk in the footsteps of Allah.*

The Process of Purification *is the process in which one can follow and elevate one's conscious level. The harmony and purification of the soul is attained by the cultivation of the intellect through the pursuit of scientific knowledge and a strict bodily discipline. This leads to the development of the mind and the purification of consciousness, which in fact, brings us closer and closer to the Father. The pursuit of scientific knowledge is important because science has truth about this physical world and helps in religion to sort through fact and fiction. Sciences explain the world we live in by using facts and experiments to prove it. For example, if you put your hand over fire it will burn your skin every time you put it over the flame. This is because of the chemical reaction to your skin as it starts to burn and this is pure science. Science is knowledge gained through experiments with normal phenomena. A strict bodily discipline is needed when you take into account that you are what you eat and how much you eat directly determines your body size and your energy levels. More on this later.*

The Atom and the Divine

Before I go further, lets talk about Atoms and how they play a major role in your consciousness. Atoms are transparent homogeneous (alike) powder consisting of an infinite number of particles. Atoms are a form of energy. Every atom is equivalent to "that which is" and the void (blackness) is equivalent to "that which is not". Atoms combine themselves for the formation of organic and inorganic world. Life and death are due to the change in the arrangement of atoms. At death the personality and senses disappear as the heavier atoms descend into the earth but the mind and soul are composed of fire atoms and ascend to the celestial regions. **Fire atoms are the finest, smoothest, and most mobile of atoms. The mind alone is self-moved and the cause of motion in everything in the universe and has supreme power over all things.** *External objects (matter) are atoms or energy that constantly giving off minute images of It's self that is turned into impressions upon our senses and set in* *motion our (fire)-atoms there by creating sensation and knowledge. Basically everything is made of energy that forms solid objects living and non-living, its just we can't see the energy it's self but only what the energy forms through the physical eye.* **Fire atoms are found all through the universe but the largest number are found in the human body**. *Since it's the mind that fills the universe only like can produce like, then the mind of the universe must have been produce by the mind that is its source, the Living Cosmic Mind known as Yahweh, the Living Light. The universe has a Living Mind controlling or overseeing what goes on within it.* **For mental growth fire atoms must rearrange themselves for new knowledge and understanding**. *The more one learns about the truth and becomes knowledgeable, the more movement or rearrangement the fire atom must go through. The more you know the faster your fire atoms move to retrieve the different knowledge from your Mental Information Processing Grid (our mini universe). One must unite all parts of your being to become one with our True Self. Through science and art you can see new things, (from old sights) through your third eye or spirit eye, which puts you in a higher position for a better view. The Egyptian's required for a first step to master one's passions, that frees up energy for the occupation of latent spiritual powers. Then search inside for the new abilities that have taking place of the old passions.* **By disciplining your mind and body you control the energies that were used blindly by your emotions and thoughts, this energy, can be redirected to give you added awareness**.

The Egyptian Ten Virtues

The ten principles virtue can, by using them from one to ten, elevate one spiritually by practicing them and begin your full control over self. Start from one and progress through to ten as your consciousness slowly opens to new perceptions and a greater advantage to see things in a different light then before. You must keep them on your mind constantly relating to the things you do or should do and say as live your life. It's never too late to make amends for something you have done but you must put forth effort to correct it. With right effort comes progress, so focus your conscious

OVERSTANDING DARKNESS

mind on thoughts that will inspire you to advance morally and intellectually. As you advance you will feel the difference as you start to gain master over your lower self.

Ten Virtues

1-CONTROLLING THOUGHT	2-CONTROLLING ACTION
3-HAVE PURPOSE – DEVOTION	4-FAITH ABILITY TO BE TAUGHT
5-FAITH IN ABILITY TO ASSIMILATE TRUTH	6-FAITH IN ABILITY TO WIELD TRUTH
7-FREE FROM RESENTMENT UNDER PERSECUTION	8-FREE FROM RESENTMENT UNDER TIMES OF BEING WRONGED
9-CULTIVATE ABILITY TO DISTINGUISH BETWEEN RIGHT AND WRONG	10-CULTIVATE ABILITY TO DISTINGUISH BETWEEN REAL AND UNREAL

1. **Control ones Thought**- First you must begin to notice thoughts stream in your mind. Try to figure out why you think the thoughts that you think. Are thought emotionally charged? You guide your thoughts to cleanse your mind from the thoughts that are not righteous and help to strengthen your conscience to get rid of evil thoughts as they enter your thought stream. When unacceptable evil thoughts pop up in your mind, the trick is, to do or think the exact opposite of it and feel the good feeling of doing that mentally or physically. Guiding ones thought is very important because you are what you think! Thought control is the foundation virtue.

2. **Control ones Action**- Don't let your emotions get the best of you by forcing or tricking you into doing something that you normally wouldn't do. Emotions cause reactions that are missing intellectual judgment. Your emotions will guide you down a path of misery and betrayal, but used correctly, can give you great

insight into not only your being but also other human feelings and thoughts (one of the gifts of the Spirit). The biggest lie one can tell is a lie to your self. The biggest fool is the one who fools himself. Control your desires and passions, that are only brought on by our emotions, and you'll be able to control your actions. There is no action done on accident because all action are made up of three components, the thought to do it, the power behind the thought (emotional or Willed), and the combination of the two is the action itself.

ACTION = THOUGHT + DRIVE (EMOTION OR WILL POWER)

Controlling thoughts and actions is derived from wisdom, for true wisdom is knowing how to act (controlling actions) and always using good judgment based on knowledge of the event or situation.

3. **Have a Devotion of Purpose**- At higher levels of consciousness there is more to life than just living to require material goods. *As one enters these higher planes of thought things like purpose and destiny make themselves known to you.* First, find your purpose in life that we all have and soon you will see that you have been working on it all the time as you examine your past. While others run from their destiny and think its too difficult because they don't really know that it brings out inner strength. The only way to find your purpose is to raise your consciousness to a level where you can overstand your life. You must look down at your self to see if you're being lead by emotions or desires or lead by the Light of Truth (Spirit). When you control your actions and thought, you are freeing up energy that was blindly being used and wasted. Now that energy is being focused back into self to raise your conscious level to realize your purpose.

4. **Have faith in the Ability to be Taught**- People don't understand much about how important having faith is. If you think you can't do something, you are locking yourself into an "I can't mode". If you think you can do something you will probably do it or keep trying till you do. You must have faith in any task you do for

it to be successful. The truth is in an individual's insperience (experienced on the inside) and it must start there before it can be externalize. If you don't believe you can be taught or have faith in the books you read (that connects to yourself) than it can't get the true meaning across to you. The teacher most time turns out to be past adventure or things in your life that molded you to be who you are today. This training comes from deep inside self and is the first sign of the personal truth that liberates use from fleshly attachments and thinking. You start to overstand more of the inner world not only in yourself but also in others.

5. **Have faith in Self to Assimilate the Truth**- The Truth at first can be very hard and cold to someone who has been lied to or is living a lie. The Truth has no feeling or regard for anyone and that's why most people when they hear the Truth either reject it or deny it. **There's no room for personal feeling in or about the Truth, it is something that one must just except when it comes to you.** As one absorbs the Truth it gets warm and it will rap itself around you protecting you from the lies of man. Everyone sooner or later, will have to become acquainted with and assimilate the Truth, for his or her progression to the next stage of consciousness either in this world or the next. The Truth is everlasting and infinite and never changes. Only our perception of the truth changes as it becomes clearer and fills us spiritually. Once you have grasps just bits of the Universal Truth it will empower you, if you follow its lead no matter where it takes you. You must not be afraid to face up to yourself, face to face in Truth. **Real Truth is only found on high spiritual levels of realization of divinity and consciousness of the communion with the Creator Spirit**. Static truth is dead truth and only dead truth can be held as a theory. Living Truth is dynamic and can enjoy experiential existence in the human mind.

6. **Have Faith in Self to Wield the Truth**- Trying to communicate the insperience that one feels to someone else can be a complicated process. Notice as you become accustomed to the truth you'll see it manifest each day in your awareness (if you focus on it).

Remember that you can't make a blind man see. Some people that you bring the true to will reject it and curse you for bringing it to them, but don't be disappointed. The more you wield the Truth the more you'll see really who wants it and who doesn't (foresight). You must wield the truth according to your level of truth and the level at which the person your communicating to can overstand it. This will take some of the shock off of it and help them to understand it less emotionally. It takes time to communicate the Truth and one must be very patient with themselves and others. Most times when the Truth is spoken to someone it shakes their foundation of what they thought Truth was. Be careful not to shake too hard as to crumble their foundation because the truth in those situation will not be accepted but hated. Make your truth loving and stable not frightening and scary. If you do shake someone's foundation you are responsible to built him or her back up again using truth.

7. **Be Free from Resentment under Persecution- As your consciousness rises you will start to see that forgiveness and love are your best weapons one can use to advance spiritually**. When being persecuted by someone else, it is their lack of peace and ignorance of Universal Law that causes him or her to treat you that way. Love can conquer hate but you must be willing to use it, especially in a world that mostly lacks compassion for others. The ones who persecutes others are to be pitied and prayed for because the Universal Law will take care of them like it takes care of you according to your intentions and actions. It does one no good to hate, or seek revenge on them because revenge is for the Creator only. Those type thoughts only bring you down to your lower nature that you trying to escape from. Virtue seven and eight are very hard to cross because of people's Ego, but you must be humble not only in the eyes of Father but also in your own eyes. Doesn't the Lord's Prayer tell us to "forgive our trespasser as we forgive those who trespass against us". At this stage the power of love begins to manifest it self as the true power of the universe and with great love comes great insight into many things, especially your fellow humans thoughts and

actions. **In essence, you exist in a "Consciousness of Death" until you are aware of the power of love that opens up the visual pathways of ascension into the indescribable levels of Light Essence (spiritual luminosity).**

8. **Be Free from Resentment under Experience of Wrong**- Like virtue seven, virtue eight, is meant to humble and strengthen the faith in the individual. All those seeking the Creator must be humbled; only through being humble can one cross the trial of persecution and that of being wronged. Together virtue seven and eight make what is called fortitude. Fortitude is having the courage under Allah's test (living righteously) and having patient endurance through the misfortune or pain because nine times out of ten it is meant to strengthen you in some way for the future. It takes spiritual insight to see and overstand why certain things happen to us. It takes love to have any insight (past the physical level) at all. We may not believe it at the time it occurs but these things that happen to us and are always for the best whether good or bad. Brought on by your own misguided deeds and by fate because it is true what doesn't kill us makes us stronger.

9. **Cultivate the Ability to Distinguish between Right and Wrong**- The aim of all spiritual cultivation should be, in one form or another, to know what is right from what is wrong. At first you may think you know (as does everyone), but as your consciousness rises what was clear and cut becomes foggy and confused. This is why to know right and wrong is so far down the virtue chain. After going through the first eight virtues, right and wrong, are totally different to you because of the love and overstanding you now possess. Finding the distinction between right and wrong may take longer than you think. Knowing the difference between right and wrong is the foundation for justice. How can one be Just without a clear view of this and our education system does not teach this. That's why judges and lawyers seem to be failing in the job to deliver justice instead its money that rules the courts. Knowing right from wrong is a

personal revelation of spirit to those in the spirit, and for those with high moral attitudes. Knowing right from wrong and doing right instead of wrong is the real lesson in virtue nine.

10. **Cultivate Ability to Distinguish between Real and Unreal**- I know some of you are thinking, what does this mean, to distinguishing between real and unreal. This is temperance (self restraint) and by practicing it you can see more clearly mentally from what is real or needed, from that what isn't real or just wanted. Sometimes we mistake a passion or desire for something that is real but it's only real in your imagination (**a blind emotional energy surge**). We think it's necessary to act a certain way or do a certain thing but it's just the confusion between real and unreal (Will power and emotional energy). Sometimes you pass a food stand and you think you are hungry, is it hunger, or are you just seeing food and wanting to eat. Is it that you were too busy to take your friend somewhere or are you just being lazy? Find the real motive for your actions and take time to think about why you do things before you express them. Unreal is the illusion that you have control over self and thinking you know, but it is just your emotions telling what you want to hear on the inside. No act or expression should be expressed when emotionally charged because they lead to crime, violence and trouble. The Creator made order, by fashioning the phenomena of matter according to the eternal prototype or ideas in perfect a manner, just as Allah created the Eloheems (and himself in the Eloheems). Things we see around us are the phenomena of nature, and belong to the earthly realm (only copies of the Divine Prototype). Ideals are things that dwell in the heavenly realms. Ideals are real and perfect, but phenomena are unreal and imperfect, just a part of the original ideal or thought. Application of philosophy enables the mind to rise above what you see and advance to the knowledge of ideal's them selves. This is saying to stop thinking and acting on a material level where things are not genuine and keep thoughts in the spiritual domain (on the real). Find Self and live in the real world that has universal love for all.

WHEN THE PHYSICAL CONDITIONS ARE RIPE, THEN SUDDENLY MENTAL EVOLUTION MAY TAKE PLACE, WHEN THE MINDS STATUS IS FAVORABLE, SUDDENLY SPIRITUAL TRANSFORMATIONS MAY OCCUR, WHEN SPIRIT VALUES RECEIVE PROPER RECOGNITION, THEN COSMIC MEANING BECOMES PERCEPTIBLE, AND INCREASINGLY THE PERSONALITY (INDIVIDUAL) IS RELEASED FROM THE HANDICAPS OF TIME AND DELIVERED FROM THE LIMITATIONS OF SPACE.

PART II   ELEVATION (FROM MAN TO GOD)

The basic man has a highly developed brain. The brain without knowledge, wisdom, and overstanding cannot elevate into a mind or intellect that could see the Light of the Universal Mind. The Light in the Mind must be sparked before any progress can be made. One must build mental energy in order to raise our consciousness level up. Mental energy and consciousness are basically equal to each other. Here are four steps to increase energy and consciousness:

ELEVATION

	BODY	EMOTION	MIND	SPIRIT
Concentration	Increases health Light absorption	Helps control your emotions reaction	Helps guide/ control thought streams	Helps reason correctly/ Calms thoughts
Meditation	Strengthened and Heals Body	Strengthens Will Power/	Strengthens mind & helps focus thought	Helps bring intuition/ Clear sight
Discipline body	Increase body energy & more energy for thought	Emotional release valve	Fights mental weakness & Strengthens determination	Increases spirit's effect on mind and body

Fasting	Heals the Body Frees energy	Fights animal urges/ weakens emotional effect	Empowers mind & Will power- destiny	Strengthens Spirit & finds the Creators Will
Scientific pursuit	Improves health & Overstanding Find what is good to eat and how to eat	Helps overstand what emotion are & realizes control over them	Feeds the mind with right Knowledge Wisdom, and Overstanding	Helps discover spiritual science and science of Self True Theology

1. **Concentration-** Start to notice when you shift the levels of your concentration each day as it rises and falls. Try to feel the energy that you use when you concentrate on something hard and when you are just having fun. As your energy level increases all sensation will have to be identified and understood. Try to notice the times when your energy changes from mental concentration to emotional and physical energies. By noticing the energy changing you can redirect it or stop it but you first must be aware of the change. Deep and focused concentration blends into meditation with breathe control.

2. **Meditation -** It is vital for humans to reflect upon his or her own mind. Meditation calms the mind by increasing the energy to soothe it. Meditation is how you find out the things that you trying to hide from yourself and finding out about your purpose and ponder about why you did something. Remember it is up to you to settle conflicts within your self because mental anguish is the worst type of pain. **Meditation is to the spirit as exercise is to the body.** Exercise your spirit to strengthen it by the use of your "Will Power" to travel into your mind, a mini universe, to clean it up and straighten it out for clear thought and added awareness. The total sum of pleasures in the world is nothing compared to the bliss derived from meditation.

3. **Discipline of the Body** - Control all body wants to get the mind ready for its discipline. Start to be aware of the how you treat your body. Do you feed it too much or not exercising it or relax it when needed. Your body size and weight have a direct relationship to your mind. If your over weight more energy is use in doing just normal every day activities (getting up in the morning, walking, breathing, blood circulation) and it takes from your mind power (you get tried easier and faster) and it hinders your consciousness. Basically you must take care of your body because that's why some people are always tired or sickly or depressed all the time. Heal your body and to start the increase in mental energy for healing your mind. Our bodies are the temples for the Spirit's Indwelling don't disrespect it, or neglect it. You are only stopping your own progress with selfishness and love of physical pleasures in excess (food, sex, drugs).

4. **Fasting** - Is one of the must helpful spiritual exercises that brings one closer to the inner Light and strengthen your mind against your desires and wants. If you can voluntarily give up food and water (or just food) from sun up to sundown for a month (or week, or days) then you can easily give up bad habits that could hinder your spiritual progression. Fasting builds mental energy because instead of running off the energy that food and water gives (or quick energy like candies), you'll be running off pure conscious energy. Keep thoughts on the Creator to strengthen you as you endure the challenge for a week to a month, several times a year. As you fast your sense of smell and taste will be enhance and your awareness of your thoughts and inner Self will become clearer. Be careful to only do what you can, don't try and do too much to soon, as you fast it will become more and more easier to do and more fulfilling. It takes a strong mind to fast from sun up to sun down for more than a few days, but that's when the struggle is the hardest. Fasting is an exercise that creates balance in the mind and body. Remember with right effort comes progress.

5. **Pursuit of Scientific Knowledge-** One must find the truth in basic science to explain the world around you. Use science to explain your body, brain, skin, people and all the things you will need to know about this mineral world as you elevate your consciousness towards the spiritual world. As ideas flood in they will need an explanation that you might not have, but by working through science you can make those perfected ideas into reality. Search for answers, on the inside of you and the outside to complete your conscious elevation, for only you can do it.

It is not enough to just understand but one must have the power to realize internally what information has to offer to truly overstand it. Everything is everything and even nothing is something. Every action has a reaction, for it sets events in motion either to have a good outcome or bad depending on your action. **Try to overstand that matter is a development of thought, crystallized mental energy**. Thought is one of the strongest weapons to fight against low desires and passion. The animal side of us must be subordinate to the higher nature or spiritual side through the way we eat, drink, think, and live.

Meditation, concentration, fasting, strict bodily discipline, and scientific knowledge will increase your mind's energy level. You must start to enhance your feeling of the inner Self, to know how to identify with the different modes of Self and stop the ones that are not good for you. For all sensations give important information if over stood. We must feel or be aware when your energy changes from mental energy to physical energy. Notice the conflicts between the feeling of right and the feeling of being wrong or doing wrong. Notice all of your feelings and wage war for what is right and help your conscience to extinguish your evil tendencies. Wage war to get control over your thinking and fight against doing something just for doing it. Make your thoughts and action in tune with your spirit. **Don't waste your thoughts and actions (energies) on low desires but use them to bring about spiritual power**. *Don't get me wrong still have fun, just work it in differently and consciously, you will enjoy yourself more because you have control over more of your being.*

<u>A balance is what is needed at all times within the various parts of your being</u>. We are all multi-dimensional beings that need control over all sides to balance our energies. Without a balanced self the confusion of energy and sensation could be quite overwhelming and lead to all kinds of destructive behavior. Balance your mind by living the ten virtues and seeking scientific knowledge to dispel the fiction from the fact. Balance your physical by not living to eat but eating to live and exercise and respect Allah's temple. Mental and physical balance helps to bring about spiritual balance and with it nothing can stand in your way.

CHAPTER III MAY BUDDHA BLESS YOU

This section of upliftment is wide spread in the eastern countries and its main message is that of the **Four Basic Truths**. *These truths may be a little harsh but one must agree that there is truth in them.*

1. All through your life there will be suffering, pain, and misery.
2. Suffering is usually caused by selfish craving and personal desires.
3. This suffering is not a necessity of life and can be over-come.
4. One way to eliminate or reduce suffering in life, that is to follow the example of "**The Eight Fold Path**".

As you can see suffering will always be proportional to your own selfish, greedy, jealous and, hateful desires that you try to fulfill. The Eight Fold Path will give you a process to curve those ill emotions and bring love and goodness back into your hearts and the hearts around you that you touch. These paths are mental exercises on the right way to think and do things personally within your daily lives. Thought is energy and right thought leads to positive energy.

THE EIGHTFOLD PATH

Right Behavior	Right Concentration	Right Speech
A. Directing thoughts	A. Controlling thought	A. Internal Awareness
B. Moral Value	B. Dedication of purpose	B. Purpose for Life
C. Internal Realization	C. Faith in own ability	C. Faith in Self
D. Controlling Actions	D. Identity with the Light	D. Truth Assimilation

Right Livelihood
A. Strong Will Power
B. Love of People
C. Destiny Realization
D. Faith in wielding truth

Right Knowledge
A. Know truth-Knowledge from relative Knowledge
B. Spiritual Cultivation
C. Pursuit of Science

Right Aspiration
A. Pursuit of Science&Math
B. Knowledge of Self
C. Self Consciousness
D. Self Discipline

Right Effort
A. Determination
B. Positive Emotion
C. Will Power to keep trying
D. Distinguishing between Right & Wrong

Right Mindfulness
A. Self Evaluation
B. Love Orientated Conscious
C. Spiritualized Mind
D. Mental Dexterous (balanced faster left/right hemisphere interaction)
E. Distinguishing between Real & Unreal

Right Knowledge- Is knowledge of what life is all about like the Four Basic Truths. Knowledge of suffering, what raises from the suffering and knowledge of the path leading to the cessation (end) of suffering. Right knowledge teaches you about self and your relation to others.

Right Aspiration - Means a clear devotion to being on the path towards enlightenment (wisdom). Aspirations for harmlessness and non-violence are right aspiration. Aspire to be Creator-like in your decisions towards others and yourself with love and mercy for all.

Right Speech - Involves both clarity of what is said and speaking kindly without malice. Which means refraining from lying, useless speech, gossip. Speak from the heart and all you say will contain positive emotion.

Right Behavior- is reflecting on one's behavior and the reason for it. Basically it means not to steal, kill, lie, or commit sexual offense. Right behavior comes from first knowing or finding out how to act. Knowing how to act comes from being spiritually connected to your Higher Spiritual Self.

<u>Right Livelihood</u>- It involves choosing an occupation that keeps an individual on the path that promotes life and well being, rather than the accumulation of money. For most of the professional occupation, this would be a problem, but remember it's not what you do but how you go about doing it that counts.

<u>Right Effort</u>- Is training the will and curbing selfish passion that places oneself along the path of enlightenment. One generates desire, effort, stirs up energy, exerts ones mind and strives to raise ones spiritual powers. With effort comes progress, no matter how slow or fast, all you need is to put the effort in the right things to succeed in life.

<u>Right Mindfulness</u>- is the continuing self-examination and self-awareness. One thinks about the body within the body, feelings within the feelings, the mind within the mind and mental states within mental states, being clearly conscious of them and mindful of them. This helps you to control the greed and depression in the world. In other words, look behind all the emotions, desires, thoughts, and likes/dislike to see who you really are, what you think you are (Human or Beast).

<u>Right Concentration</u>- Is being absorbed into the state of bliss. By reducing aimless thought, with the mind subjectively tranquilized and fixed on one point. One can enter in and remains in a meditation state that's empty of thought and born from concentration that's energetic. This is the aim of all spirits and humans to enter this state of heavenly bliss.

Ascending and descending Creations

Perfect creations---The ALL----Perfect Unity **Descending Creation - Perfectly created**

Involution Spiritual **beings descend to create life in Lower realms** Mental **Evolution in the Image of the Creator (Humans)**

Emotional

Physical

<u>Ascending Creations</u>- Imperfect creation ascending towards perfection (level by level)

Descending Creations- (Going down from Perfection to Create)

Perfect Creations--
--------------Involution

Conscious of Spiritual Matters--------------Involution - whole principles brakes down

Heavenly Planes

Mental Planes

Earthly Planes

Conscious of Physical Matter-----------------------------Evolution - Parts built upwards

Imperfect Creations---
---------------Evolution

Ascending Creations (Ascend to become perfect)

There are two forces in the universe, one that is of creation and, the other is that of destruction. The universe and all matter in the universe will go from a higher order (the One) to a lower order (the many). Now physical life goes from lower orders of humans to higher orders of angelic being. The law of the all binds the evolutionary process of everything. Evolution is the creation of a more complex life form from less complex life forms. If you keep your thoughts on the universal matters of science and goodness you will elevate yourself to a position of holiness within your spirit. Let the Light of your soul be your guide. Evil is a condition that can only exist when good does nothing. Good is the Light of creative action and evil is the darkness of inaction. Where there is no good, there is only evil and where there is no light, there is only darkness. This is a fundamental truth. <u>You must work your way up the ladder of life until you reach a point that your spiritual enlightenment is so great that there no physical life forms complex enough to contain you.</u> The more advanced you become, the more you will be able to create. You are the sum of your action (or intentions), it is by them alone, that you may gauge your own spiritual level. You are the only one responsible for your spiritual development. **To be amongst**

the creators you must create and one simple good deed is an act of creation. Love is the most powerful tool that a creator can use because the universe is sustained by the love emanation of the Father being spread out by the Son and bestowed on humans by the Infinite Spirit.

You will see that once you have attained all the enjoyment that can be afforded by intellectual progress, one will perceive that he has not obtained complete happiness, and that complete happiness is impossible without security in social relation. One can only obtain this security through the moral progress of society in general; the force of things will lead one, to labor for that end and to the attainment of which this doctrine will furnish you with the means. **REMEMBER THIS:**

LOVE IS, UNDERSTANDING UNDERSTANDING IS ENERGY, ENERGY IS, POWER, POWER IS, A FORCE, THIS FORCE GIVES ONE, CONTROL, NOT OVER OTHERS BUT CONTROL OVER SELF, WITH LOVE FOR SELF BRINGS KNOWLEDGE OF SELF

CHAPTER 4 SENSORISM AND MELANIN

*As I said earlier in my introduction that melanin tunes you into cosmic energies. These energies can be absorbed and utilized as one starts to reach the higher consciousness levels. Before I start talking about melanin, first let me start to explain about our total awareness system (includes mind, body, soul, all senses and power in them) that we'll call SENSORISM. Your **sensorial system** is your entire sensory apparatus, consciousness and awareness, emotions of the body, unconsciousness, and psychic attraction and repulsion of the mind. To make things clearer here's some quick definition:*

1. **Sensory Receptors** detects signals (light/energy) and enter the signals into your sensorial system to be identified and then converted into feeling, perception and, impression that interact with one's intellect.

2. **Sensory Transducers** is a mechanism that converts one form of energy (light/signal) into another form that can be utilized by different systems (glands) in your body.

3. **Sensibility** is a peculiar sensitivity to a pleasurable or painful impression like feeling or moods of others. (Impression are internal)

4. **Sense** is the faculty of externally being aware of something in your environment. When something is sensed it is smelled, touched, seen, heard or, tasted. (External)

The difference in sense and sensibility is that sensibility involves impressions which are internal and senses processes direct sensory data from the environment or externally.

Our sensory receptors input various internal and external signals into a vast complex sensory system. Inputted signals need to be transduced into different forms in order to be utilized by the sensorial system. In other words, the signal or energy get changed or refined so that your sensory system can use it. Your sensory system then feeds it into your bodily system, glands, and mind. The human sensorial system possesses a hard drive faculty or tools to construct an enormous variety of sensory transducers. These transducers are only constructed as a result from repeated exposure to signals in some kind of cognitive (mental) way. Since your sensorial system is unceasingly being bombarded with countless signals from the cosmos, your sensory transducer only appears when the intellect recognizes a need or use for them. If you take the five senses for example, they are sensory receptors for external stimuli and are necessary and automatically developed. We really don't have five senses anyway, just one, touch which is multiplied by deception to five. For to see light, it must touch nerve centers in the eyes, to smell particles must touch the nerve centers in the nose, to hear sound waves must touch nerve centers in the ear, and to feel and taste particles must touch the tongue or skin. These sensory receptors that make up the five senses are really gross sensory receptors. They inform us of the tangible or heavier form of energy (matter). Tangible things can only be experienced locally in your physical vicinity. We also have subtle sensory receptors to inform us of the finer forms of energy or intangible things. They inform us of energies of the spirit and messages of light (immaterial). The intangible can be experience non-locally (signals come from everywhere) and is not dependent on the physical vicinity. These internal signals puts us closer to the Divine Self within each human being as the invisible world becomes partially known or visible in the spiritualize mind.

MATTER /GROSS /TANGIBLE /MATERIAL = SPIRITUAL/ FINE/ INTANGIBLE/ IMMATERIAL

Melanin is a transducer of both material and spiritual energies. Melanin is a transducer of intangible energy sources and the subtle sensory receptors that connect one with the spiritual energy of the universe. *The pale people have a melanin deficiency that doesn't allow them full contact as the people with massive amounts of melanin have. The more melanin one has, the more contact you will be able to feel from the universe because melanin is the solid form of light on earth. This relationship between*

OVERSTANDING DARKNESS

the intangible subtle energy and transducers has to be developed in people without melanin in their skin, much more than people with it, to feel the universal energies. The development of your intangible transducers doesn't happen in all peoples because most distance themselves from the intangible by thinking only in material ways (energy follows thought). No working relationship between your transducers has been established to the lighter energies except the automatic one that melanin gives, but most people are not aware of this. As you raise your consciousness level the more subtle sensory transducers will be formed to process the new energy. The more one focuses one senses into the physical, it permits the shameful (lower animal nature) formats of behavior, which is so common amongst Americans of today. It gives the illusion that we are separate entities and this gives way to the worst kinds of emotion like selfishness and greed. This is why there is so much violence and crime going on in the world today because people have been focused on the tangible and material (money, cars, houses) instead of developing their subtle or immaterial perceptions mainly through meditations. **The introduction to the subtle intangible energies brings beneficial change in behavior based on the principle that human behavior works according to the limits of what they perceive. The spiritual energies give rise to moral and ethical development.** *You will start to feel what is real from the unreal and what is right from wrong. Things will be clearer as you develop the transducers to overstand these subtle energies. This is why melanin puts people with it throughout their skin in tune with each other because melanin is a divine gift from Allah to keep our spirits strong under persecution of this earthly test. This is why it is harder for pale people to feel the divine guide that cultivates their righteousness and goodness. It's easier for them to be selfish and conceitful because they think they are all alone, separate from everyone else. Some of our pale brothers and sister have a moral center and they have been exposed to situations that make subtle transducers form but most have not.* **The physical senses are made up of an array of sensory receptors that receive these energies, from the environment, that are converted into what we see, hear, and perceive.** *The conversion takes place till the process comes to include information* *loads that are invisible to the five senses. We are dealing with an array of increasingly specialized sensory transducers that deal with information that are not drawn from contact with one's local environment. These signals of energy are always hitting our sensory receptors and some races have more transducers to bring in more meaning than other races.* <u>*The more information or meaning one can interpret, or is aware of, the higher states of consciousness that one individual can perform on.*</u> *The reason why you are unaware of this process is that, it happens so quickly (in the blink of an eye), and is so normal that must people don't realize what is really going on. The five senses are useless if their sensory inputs are analyzed by the intellect. Then it seems to depend on the loads of information accumulated and activity contained in the intellect, at the individual level, to bring the energy into meaning. In other words, what good are the senses if your mind doesn't have a working knowledge on how to get information from them? This is why two people can see the same situation happen in front of there eyes and both give a different account on what they saw. One or both of them could be wrong if they have not formed the correct transducers, the information they received will give them a incorrect evaluation of the situation.* <u>*What we call the five physical senses aren't really senses at all but actually there are made up of extraordinary complex interaction amongst vast number of sensory receptors*</u>*. These interactions involve the electromagnetic level of the behavior of atoms that comprise our molecules and cells. The function of our bio-organic materials, the synapse, chemical electrons comprising our nervous system (brains, as well as in our sensorial system's energy field (aura) are all a part of the vast number of sensory receptors. The arrays of receptors that receive the signals are inputted into our sensorial systems as waves, frequencies, and vibration. They are then transduced and outputted into the cognitive consciousness that transduces it further into a form of meaning, at which points of the signal can be recognized.*

    The full spectrum of light, when personified in the physical state manifests as blackness. This means when all forms of light are combined they would appear black. Another reason why melanin is so important is because on the planet earth the **solid form of light is melanin (forth dimensional plasma)**. *However when the visible* *spectrum of light appears, it manifests as white light. Humans on this planet who are pale skinned are reflecting light, instead of absorbing light, which comes from our visible light spectrum. This is why pale people sunburn so easily. Their thin pale skin has no defense against the ultraviolet rays that come through the ozone layer. Sunburn damage is permanent and is irreversible. When people with melanin throughout their skin absorb sunlight their skin gets thicker because melanin is produced to work hand in hand with the suns light.* **Even before the creation of the earth melanin rich black skin has provided the physical body with the best protection from exposure, disease, and the best contact with ones Higher Self and the Solar System**. *This is why the people with the strongest hormones, black people, are called "the Sun People". The ultraviolet rays from the sun destroy the cells in the outer layer of the skin, of people without massive amount of melanin in their skin, and causes damage to their tiny blood vessels underneath. This is what causes the many forms of skin cancer in whites. The pale skin turns red and may blister and this causes malignant melanoma that is responsible for the three to four times as many deaths a year as non-melanoma skin cancer. In 1992 1,142 people in Britain died of melanoma and over the last ten years there has been 50% increase in the pale people dying from malignant melanoma. In 1994, 4,438 new cases of malignant melanoma were diagnosed (2,722 women: 1716 men) in the UK. Skin cancer in the UK has more than 40,000 new cases a year and about 1,800 deaths per year. The people, who reduce the importance of melanin, are those individuasl with the least amount of melanin, but they are only hurting their own people. The people with melanin in Africa, India, and Australia have deposits of melanin in the skin the heaviest because of the intense sunlight. Northern Europeans have the least amount in their skin and are lighter because of the cool and cloudy weather. The thickness of the outer layer of the skin is also a factor, for people with darker skin complexions have thicker layers of skin that enhances the skins filtering effect. In the thinner pale skin, the blood vessels show through and give a pinkish color and are easily penetrated by the ultraviolet rays of the sun. The sun gives people, which can absorb the light, vitamins and nutrients.* Melanin is like a super conductor, or like a car battery in a car, that stays charged when it is exposed to light, sound, and colors of energy (signals). It will absorb the energy to the point where melanin will actually recharge itself to a brand new level. **Melanin is also a transducers of sound and light which occurs inside the body of the blacks, this is why when people with massive amounts of melanin hear good music it make them move, the energy from the music is actually charging on the inside of their body** *(bouncing around inside them) giving the feeling to move and dance that's the expression of rhythm and soul. Melanin also acts as a computer, controls growth rate and sleep cycle, reacts to gravity, and protects blacks from extreme hot and cold. Music is transduced by the melanin in the skin that keeps the tempo inside of our bodies. The music can't be transduced to vibrate inside bodies with pale skin. People with massive amounts of melanin in their skin still hear the beat after its gone off because melanin gets charged from audio waves as well as from light.*

Anatomy of Whites and Blacks

Blacks	*Whites*
Melanin high content-- increase color, sound and light absorption	*Least amount causes Albinism*
Skin Melanin Rich	*Skin Albinism - Lack of Melanin in skin*
Buttocks high in muscular development	*Flat Buttocks*
Hair- least amount on body cause by melanin's insulating effect	*Predominantly hairy*
Hair - curly and brown that allows quicker transmission in receiving electrical and magnetic energies like antenna	*Hair- flat and limp forms weak antenna*

Eye's - brown that allow better reception of sun's color-light-heat-results in a higher stimulation of Pineal & Pituitary Glands	Albinism causes eye's to be many colors They see paler color/ blinded by the sun
Nerves- High melanin content in nervous system that allows nerve messages to travel faster and protects against disease	Nerves very little melanin
Stomach - has Flora - fungi, Yeast virus, and bacteria- that lives in stomach and entire digestive tract (Also in eyes, ears etc. and is specific to blacks only About 3 pounds in body) Allow for food breakdown (Metabolizes) at a greater nutritional level	Stomach - Can't handle vast variety of food that limits food Metabolism
Skin - absorbs greatest percentage of colors	Skin reflects colors
Breathe- deeper Characteristic of right-minded thinking	Shallow breathe Characteristic of left-minded thinking

Taken from African Holistic Health 4th Edition by Dr.Imhotep Llaila O.Afrika

The wavelength frequency of energy in pale people's skin can be measured at 400 to 700 manometers ($1 \times 10^{-9}=$ one times ten to the power of -9) this is the frequency of light their body is made out of. The longer the wave frequency the more amount of energy the wave has. Since the pale skin has such a low wave length it reflects the long wave frequency back off of their pale skin. The wave length frequency for Nubian vibrates from 000.1 miles to 3100 miles. What a difference! Since the black skin has such a long wave frequency it can absorb the shorter frequencies of light (energy), *which melanin is made out of, which the visible light operates on. The cosmic rays are the shortest in wavelength and the longest are those of electricity. Since the ozone layer holds back most of the shorter cosmic rays and only lets in certain kinds which are longer rays like radio waves and visible light. The ozone layer by the way is not as damaged like they say it is. For most of the scientist today say the ozone is but the earths atmosphere will always keep a balance for us to live. This hole in the ozone layer could be letting the excess carbon dioxide out of the atmosphere into space to keep balance.* At the magnetic north and south pole is where the comic rays from outer space pour onto the earth and the excess CO2 escapes back into space. These cosmic rays are what keeps the earth's balance in energy and keeps us in the correct environment to live. *The earth is heating up because we are going into a new faze, into the solar cycles of our solar system, which pushes all the planets closer to the sun. We are leaving the lunar cycle and the earth magnetic fields are shifting to new position and it's all a part of the galactic movement.*

The white people don't receive the energy that the people with melanin in their skin do. Inside the energy we receive subtle cosmic connection that makes people clothed in melanin act so different than those people without it. Melanin is divine! **_Melanin has chemical and physical properties, not to mention personality traits (caring, loving, forgiving) and these personality traits are what make melanin different from all other chemicals_**. *The blackness of melanin makes up the color in everything on the earth (hair, plants, animal), but there are thousands of properties that make its uniqueness, besides color. It is an extremely stable molecule, meaning it is highly resistant to digestion by most acids and its bases are hard to analyze. Due to the fact that scientist can't brake melanin down.* Only a little functional melanin is needed to organize an entire cell or an entire neural system. *This is why good music makes people with melanin feel great because melanin processes the energy (sonic vibration) into feeling and sensation. In hair that turns gray melanin is dead and this is a sign of health because the first indication of disease or old age shows in*

OVERSTANDING DARKNESS

the wrinkling of the skin and color of the hair as the melanocytes (cell that produce melanin) die. There are different textures of hair vary from six ether to nine ether depending on the amount of blackness (melanin) a person has. Ether determines the amount of melanin a race has or doesn't have.

Six ether means that the hair is straight and thin (animal hair) and has six points of melanin. **Seven Ether** has wavy hair and has seven points of melanin and hair goes from thin, at the roots, to thick. **Eight Ether** has seven and half points to eight points of melanin and the hair curly, going from thick, at the roots, to thin. **Nine Ether** is kinky (or kingly) hair thats thick all the way from the root on out and has nine points of melanin (found in Nubian's only). The Egyptian pharaoh's had Nine Ether; it was a gift from the Eloheems (God Body). Kinky hair is really kingly hair do to its unique quality. The texture of hair is a sign of your hormone strength or weakness. Nine Ether seen when the hair follicles are in the ninth setting of nine in your head. Nine Ether is only produced by the life given, burning energy that the sun produces. We were made this way for the best contact with universal energies.

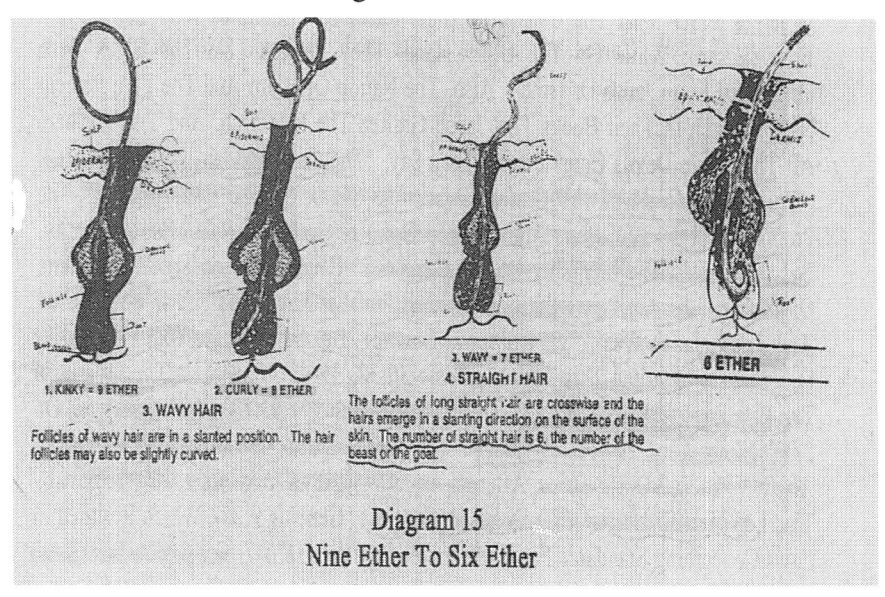

Diagram 15
Nine Ether To Six Ether

Nine ether means 9 to the 9th power of nine that originated for the triple stage of darkness. **Nine Ether represents the original Creator who grew the universe.** It stands for the three abodes heaven, hell, and creation. Ether, a conscious gas that gives moral judgment, awareness, and conscience that is made from all the existing gases in the universe (nothing is stronger than all the gases in the universe that forms the planets). Blacks carry these strong hormone traits. **Ether comes from the sun's genes, its life giving genes that shows in the hair follicle. Nine Ether Hair is set in the ninth setting of nine deep into the skull. Nine points of melanin are a divine gift from the Eloheem's to their children, evolutionary descendants to upgrade our evolution, pass other races, and the reason for our persecution.** Nine Ether is the power of reason and the most potent power in the universe that was placed in the follicle of all Nubians. The New Being race or Melanin-ite Children are descendants of the original creative forces of the universe.

Basic make-up of Melanin

Melanin is the most primitive, and universal in pigmentation in living organisms. Melanin is produced by the Pineal gland, which is the master gland of the body that controls the Pituitary Gland that controls all other glands (directly or indirectly). *In each and every living organism that aids the body melanin appears like eyes and ears of the nervous system. There are different types of melanin like brain melanin called neuro-melanin, skin melanin, and melanocytes are the epidermal cells capable of synthesizing and arranging melanin in the skin. Melanin controls all mental and physical activities in the people with it in large amounts. The melanin that's throughout our body is the same property that colors the planet earth and all genes, all creatures on the earth have melanin and are coated with it from simple organisms like fungi to the more advanced like primates. Melanin is the finest of the refined chemicals known to our species.* A metal ion acts as a backbone for the polymer structure of melanin, resulting in a metal-organic complex (network). This complex metal compound is the only substance in the body that is an organic semi-conductor. Melanin has an energy gap for the absorption of energy that makes it increase in its conductivity and sensitivity to the electromagnetic world of Etheric Being, in astral projection and, to Spiritual Entities. *In other words, energy can pass through melanin just like electricity through water or steel but in melanin the energy actually charges melanin like a car battery for the body. This is how the Egyptians kept their dead remains from decay by electrifying the mummy's skin to keep its melanin alive. The Egyptians did this because they new that the body of Africans contains massive amount of melanocytes that encode all life experience in their melanin production. Melanin actually creates an actual reality state after death. By electrifying the skin to keep the melanin alive was supposed to enhancing one position in the spirit world by keeping the link between the melanin (the physical) and spirit alive.* **Melanin is the solid form of light on earth**.

Melanin has black and brown granules (particle) that act as tiny primitive eyes that form a large neural network (sensorial system) structure to absorb and decode (transduce) electromagnetic waves. *These* **small eyes of melanin granules** *are what keep Africans from being sickly. They automatically send messages to your body saying where the damage has occured and help in the healing process. Melanin is important because it is an oxidized form RNA, which enables the body to produce proteins for cellar repair or damaged DNA. In other words, when you cut your self you have damaged your DNA (body structure) and melanin aids in healing it back to normal.* Black skin is composed of layers of organic semiconductor (melanocytes) that can be considered as forth dimensional. Ninety five percent of matter in the universe is in this state of plasma or forth-dimensional matter. Since melanocytes are the basics of higher mental activity (consciousness), it stands to reason that the people with massive amounts of melanin, have a moral nature that's more directly in contact with the Creator through the spirit. *If the resonant frequency of melanin was known, the appropriate energy could be absorbed through the skin to revitalize it and delay aging process. This is how the Ancient Egyptians were able to pre-long their own life.*

In conclusion, melanin is more than anyone could imagine it to be. With melanin, the key to blackness is in your minds. When overstanding blackness is in your hands, you will acquire the Knowledge of Self, and raise your consciousness level (energy level). How many ills do we owe to the excess of our ambitions and the indulgence of our passions? One who should live soberly (seriously) in all respects, who never runs into excess of any kind, who is always simple in his/her tastes and, modest in his desires, would escape a large proportion of tribulations of human life. It depends on each of us to free ourselves from the influence of matter on our action in your life. Let one conquer ones animal passion; let one rid self of the hatred, envy, jealously, pride and, throw off the yoke (shell) selfishness by cultivating noble sentiments. Do good and attach to things of this world only the degree of importance that they deserve. Use melanin for its purpose. For those who don't have massive amounts of melanin, you can still receive universe energies but in a different ways, it just takes effort and patience. No one is closed to spirituality unless they choose to be.

CHAPTER 5 BREATHE- THE KEYS TO YOUR ENERGIES

To breathe is to live. When something is breathing it is alive and all beings on the earth need to breathe. Even fish breathe in oxygen through the water. **Air is a form of energy for the body.** *When you run you breathe in more air (energy) because you need it for all the physical exertion you are doing. Whenever the body needs energy, controlled breathing, is good way of getting it. The muscle in your stomach called the diaphragmatic muscle controls breath. Breath control is one of the most important doctrines to come out of Egypt. By controlling your breath you can manipulate your focus of consciousness. Within meditation one can focus it or unfocused it at will. Your consciousness has two fundamental modes, with three sets in each mode. Your consciousness has in it six modalities (styles, ways).*

1. "**Being Asleep**" is a modality (form) of the **introverted state of consciousness**. The focus of energy is inside of self.
    1A. Introverted state can be focused / awake /active
    2A. Introverted state can be focused /awake /relaxed
    3A. Introverted state can be unfocused /asleep

2. "**Being Awake**" is a modality of the **extroverted state of consciousness**. The focus of energy is on the outside in the environment and surroundings.
    1B. Extroverted state can be focused / awake / active
    2B. Extroverted state can be focused /awake / relaxed
    3B. Extroverted state can be unfocused / asleep

Extroverted B

1B. *Awake - focused and active extroverted state. Focus on the environment and being active part of it. (Participating in it).*

2B. *The meditation state of consciousness is focused but mentally relaxed and more receptive. The state for learning or reading.*

3B. *The heights of the mediumistic trance (deep meditation and strong thought) like a Willed daydream but being lost in the vision.*

Introverted A

1A. *Focus is introverted (focus inside mind) so we detach our consciousness from the environment and body still remains awake and active.*

2A. *Focus of attention is detach from our environment and body yet remaining awake (Will is focus), but mentally passive. In this state the life force is free to associate thought with spiritual agencies, deities, and ancestors are able to enlighten the meditator.*

3A. *Unfocused Introverted state or better known as sleeping. Detachment from the environment and unfocusing of the Will is the undirected stream of imagery call dreaming. That's is why there sometime so hard to remember because your not really focusing on them.*

The introverted state of consciousness in all modes reduces the receptivity to distraction of the environment by focusing all attention on the inner thought and images. This also reduces the activity of the left side of the brain (part associated with numbers and letters) and increases the right side of the brain (the part associated with pictures and images). **Memory is the chief function that works best with what is seen rather than what is heard. Meditation depends primarily on visual over verbal thinking.**

When consciousness is extroverted, thus communicating with the environment and the body sensation, the will is in a passive state. We tend to fall into a mediumistic trance. A mediumistic trance is like a deep daydream, or like being asleep with your eyes open. It's like being in-between consciousness and the subconscious at the same time (self hypnoses). The individual is guided in meditation or trance state by the spirit or by the will of another (hypnotist, deity). This is known as possession when coming from a spirit, deity, or

OVERSTANDING DARKNESS

ancestor and obsession when the direction is coming from a highly charge passion (this is how your emotions/desires control you). **In a mediumistic trance, the Will doesn't control thought, the Wills function is to direct how thoughts come together for making meaningful units in conformity (harmony) to logical principle, facts, and truth.**

PART II RESTRAINED BREATHING (PRANAYAMA)

Manifestations of thought, as well as sensation (emotions), are to be controlled by the manipulation of the diaphragmatic muscles. *This set of muscles located in the lower abdomin (stomach) an inch below the navel, where we derive our physical and moral strength. At moments when you're fighting or playing, right before you get hit, you automatically tighten this stomach area. You instinctively summon strength in this manner. You can also wipeout thought and negate emotions too. This is based on your taking a deep breathe while pushing out on the lower abdomen (a pop belly) then tightening the diaphragmatic muscles while releasing breathe (called restrained breathing). While doing this you must ignore other thoughts that tend to rise up and the emotional energies will disappear. Summoning strength is incompatible with the thinking process. The two activities operate on opposite psycho-physical setting, so when you need to summon strength in a crisis, don't think, just act, because thinking takes too long when you only have a split second to react. The tension of diaphragmatic breathing is the key to concentrating the attention and summoning strength from the spiritual, mental, or the physical. The essence of breathing is the handling of the out breathes.*

Breathe guideline

First take a deep breathe pushing the abdomen muscle out to full expansion (pop belly). Secondly, as you breathe out, pull in (tighten) the abdomen muscle just below the navel, and then release breath without releasing the tension. The result is a restrained exhalation in which the lower abdomen is contracted (squeezed). This is the essence of Pranayama! Prana is an ancient technique of extracting and retaining energy from the air. In those karate and kung-fu tournaments, when they break wood or cement with their bare hands, this is the technique they were using to gather their strength. They would intake a full amount of air, then tighten their abdomen muscle and exhale. They will keep doing this still they have enough energy (air) built up to explode in a force to break the object. When meditation is conducted with this mode of breathing, it becomes an automatic activity as the meditator enters into a trance. In this state of trance anything in the physical or spiritual worlds are attainable to the meditator. You should seek to carry out all goals in or through a trance, as it is the vehicle of perfection because it uses the subconscious mind to change behavior. By carrying out the goal or objective in a meditative state that will make an impression on your spirit (subconscious) as to what you need or want to accomplish. This is done by manipulation of breathe in such a manner as to induce a state of trance then the spirits' power of omniscience or subconscious comes into being. When the spirit continues this form of restraint breath automatically, the power of the spirit to achieve is fully awakened. Use this power for fulfilling goals and for spiritual cultivation of your soul. You can also heal yourself by meditation. When you meditate deeply you are using a thousand times more energy then in your normal awakened state. It is like you are running or playing basketball but all the energy is focused on the inside. The energy alone will heal you if you're consistent in your meditations. **Meditation is for the spirit what exercise is for the body**.

PART III **THE PHYSIOLOGICAL BASIS AND BREATHE RATE**

When applying tension to the lower abdomen during meditation, it presses against the pnemo-gastric nerve, which is the main nerve of the parasympathetic division of the nervous system that decreases activity like going to sleep at night. By pressing on the pnemo-gastric nerve this stimulates it to higher activity. As this activity inhibits the sympathetic division of the nervous system, that increase activity, which is in charge of externalizing consciousness and preparing us for external action. Consciousness can also be withdrawn into

OVERSTANDING DARKNESS

the inner plane and still use the sympathetic division of the nervous system but only its wakefulness part (awaken you fully to the inner plane). *The pnemo-gastric nerve stimulation sends nervous impulses (energy/signals) to the wakefulness part of the nervous system that in turn, excites the cerebral cortexes, contributing to the increase of activity (energy) to these higher brain functions. In others words, you would be using enough energy to run ten miles but all of it is focused inside your soul to travel to different planes within your own mind or your mini universe. This is what causes the healing process to take place because now your body has more energy that's shooting through it and it can take what it needs.*

The rate at which we breathe is the key controls to our consciousness being externalized or internalized. *When you concentrate intensely you hold your breath automatically. Like when reading this is an instinctive act to withdrawn the consciousness from physical plane to focus on the mental plane. It also slows down thought activity. The normal breathe rate is about eighteen breathes per minute. When you are concentrating heavily or study hard your breath rate drops to about nine breathe per minute. At eighteen breathes per minute (which is 6+6+6) is the sign of the Beast 666. At this rate emotions easily can control you and evil tends to influence peoples thoughts. When breathing at nine breathes per minute you may run into sleepiness because of the intake of air (energy) has diminished and it puts you into what's near a trance state. That's why when you study real hard or read a book for a long time or even when watching a movie you sometimes fall a sleep, because you are so relaxed consciously. That's why you sometimes can remember or imagine the book or a movie inside your mind. The meditator can lower the breathe rate to 7.5 breathe per min. or 6, 4.5, 3, 1, each rate slowly tunes us in higher levels of conscious experience.*

Breathe Chart

Breathes per Minute----------------------------Length of wave form

1 breathe = 1 wave-----1 wave = 4 pulses

18 breathes per min- 666- Shallow breathe-Animal Breathe-Emotionally controlled-Causes selfish behavior-low external consciousness	18 waves per min or 72 pulses per min Wave form
9 breathes per min - Full breathe - Heals - Good for concentration and reading- Causes elevated consciousness and internal awareness	9 waves per min or 36 pulses per min Wave form
7.5 breathes per min - Energy breathe - draws in vibrations- - Good for mantra repetition- Causes high conscious awareness	7.5 waves per min or 30 pulses per min Wave form
6 breathes per min - Good for learning and memorizing-- Overstanding and realizing	6 waves per min or 24 pulses per min Wave form
4.5 breathes per min - To Overstanding spiritual truths - with limited use of ones omniscience	4.5 waves per min or 18 pulses per min Wave form
3 breathes per min - for intuition and stopping thought flow - Full use of omniscience	3 waves per min or 12 pulses per min Wave form
1 breathes per min - to Inperience Pure Love - merging into the Light Essence	1 wave per min or 4 pulses per min Wave form

All things living vibrate at their own specific vibration rate. The vibrating mechanisms of the human body are controlled by the breath system. *At rest the spirit vibrates 18 waves per minute or 25,920 breaths or waves per day but during meditation it is slowed and the spirit vibration is tuned into different level of energy. Remember that the larger the wave pulse the more energy that is in it, by reducing your breath you tune into strong waves of energy. The ratio between the breath rate and pulse rate is 1 to 4 (18 breathes to 72 pulses per minute). The earth's rotation on its axis is one degree every four minutes. A ratio of one to four is a good meditation objective and will tune you into the earth's rotational rate.*

When you breathe at **one breathe per minute** *you will make contact with your divine nature and the love of the universe. When you breathe at* **three breathes per minute** *all things stop like thought and the ability to intuit (use intuition) all the knowledge one needs from one omniscience part of our higher faculties. This also heals the body and prolongs life because of the energy inputted at this state of consciousness. When* **breathing at four and half breathe per minute** *you will get the overstanding of the spiritual truth but is at limited use of your omniscience. Breathing* **at six breathes per minute** *is excellent for learning new information and memorizing facts. Breathing* **at seven and half breathes per minute** *is the rate good for performing the protracted (prolong) repetition of the mantras (words of power). Breathing* **at nine breaths per minute** *is the rate excellent for strengthening the body and correcting certain illness, disease, and feebleness. When you are* **breathing at eighteen breathes per minute** *is the rate we are externalized and fully subject to the domination of thought and emotions. This is the rate that the beast (animal spirit/ low self) within uses to live. Control the breast by denying its breathe.*

Michael Campbell

The Lungs and breathing chart

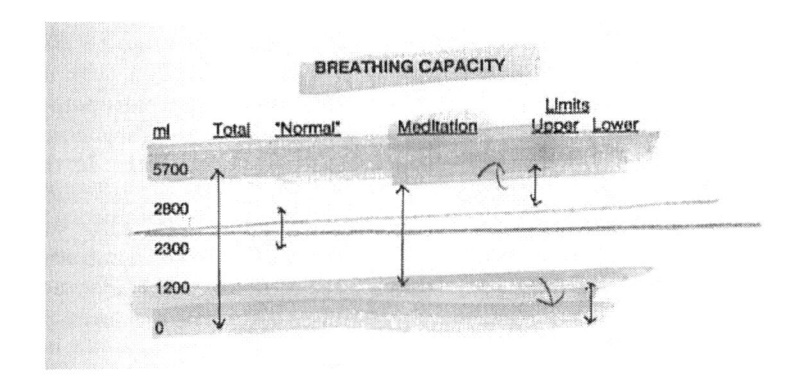

ml	Total	"Normal"	Meditation	Limits Upper Lower
5700				
2800				
2300				
1200				
0				

BREATHING CAPACITY

*The total capacity of the lungs is 5700 millimeters of air. We normally take in 500 ml of air varying between 2300 millimeters and 2800 millimeters. You have two upper sets of lungs and to two lower sets of lungs both with a special job. The lower lungs hold about 1200 ml of air and the upper lungs hold about 2900 ml of air. You can't expel all of the carbon dioxide in the lower lung and you can't fill the upper lungs with air to its full amount either. The problem is, that at our **normal breath of 500 ml of air (energy -that varies between 2300-2800ml) is called a shallow breath that causes health problems, and failure to perform to our mental optimum, and develop spiritually**. When you meditate or exercise vigorously you use up to 1700 ml of air, either focused on the muscle exertion (exercise) or used to fully awaken us in meditation. The extra 1200 ml of air taken in and expelled is above the normal 500ml and when mediating it fully awakens us.* <u>Our normal state of awareness is not one of full wakefulness, it is a blend of thought direction (Willed activity) and perception with the passive following of thought drift (dreaming). Clear perception will reveal that we dream while awake and while asleep.</u> *It's the thought drift (day dreams) that leads consciousness astray. Some try to use logic or definition to stand for realities that self is trying to gain knowledge of. Let me explain another way. Like I said you don't have two lungs in you body but four lungs working for you.*

Lungs picture

Your doctor will say it's the left and the right lungs but that's not detailed enough when you look at how breathe control is used you have to say the upper pair and lower pair of lungs. There are two different categories to breathing and most people breathe the wrong way.

1. **Shallow breathing**- is when you breathe primarily from the upper set of lungs which means you are not getting the proper amount of air needed for optimum mental operations. You know if you breathe this way, because as you breathe your shoulders and chest expand slightly forward on each in breath. This is an incomplete breath because the air (energy) is not filling all four lungs. The less air (energy) in the body, per breath, and you fall susceptible to emotion easier and fall into thought drafts (dreams). Your civilizing brain (Cerebrum) does not get the proper amounts of air/energy that it should, so it can't control the lower brain, like it should.

2. **Full breathing**- is when you breathe from the lower set of lungs that automatically fills the upper set with the proper amount of air (energy). Then you can breathe out the air in the upper set of lungs having left the proper amount of air in the lower set of lungs. You will know when you breath is complete because your abdomen will fill with air and it will be expanded (pop belly) when you breathe in air and will fall when you expel carbon dioxide. It is a subconscious thing that you have program your self to do automatically, if you don't already. The only people that would breathe correctly will be those who depend on breathe for there jobs like runners, playing instrument, swimmers, and anything that involves breathing correctly or the holding of breathe. They

are educated slightly on the importance of correct breathing so they perform it subconsciously or normally.

When a individual gets excited in a tense or emotionally charged situation they tend to hyperventilate. Hyperventilation is shallow breathing, caused by an intense emotion and that emotion causes a rapid heart beat that throws off the rhythm of breath and starts off rhythm breathing. The mixture of output and input of air is not correct, and this is why some people pass out, do to the lack of carbon dioxide in the body and the over abundance of oxygen. When hyperventilating the thought drift (daydreams) seems so vivid and real that they lead consciousness astray. *People try to use logic in their daydreams (illusion) that's overwhelming them with emotional energies and they get dazed and pass out. There is a process for everything and the answers are out there but you must raise your consciousness to see them. Breathing correctly is a must if you want to master your lower self. Swallow breathing can cause sickness in some and it stops others from participating sports and exercising properly. When exercising some get a pain in their kidneys and think there is something wrong with them, but it's just there breathing. It is funny that just a simple thing like breathing can be so important to your health and how conscious one is. You can use breath control in studying and for a better memory, because memory is a function of energy waveforms. By controlling your breath you will be more receptive to the information and have more energy to turn information into Self Knowledge. By linking information to something already understood you will be able to recall it when you recall the thing that you associated the information with. Complete breathing will sort the confusion (thoughts moving too quickly) when you use the pranayama technique. The combination of tension at the lower abdomen with the increase intake and expulsion of air will fully awaken you, and your awareness is increased. The sphere of awareness (mind) is emptied of thoughts leaving you free to handle any situation. In this state you can:*

1. Look into the nature of things and reality
2. Think (string thoughts together) logically and analogously (similarly) without loosing concentration.
3. Concentrate your attention on the words of power, Mantra's / hekeu's.
4. Insperience the reality for our self, and the formless unmanifested reality (spiritual reality).

PART IV THE TWO HEMISPHERE'S OF THE CEREBRUM (BRAIN)

Breathing has a direct effect on the brain and which hemisphere one uses. Like I said before one must consciously control the brain stem and the mid brain with the civilizing brain of the cerebrum. When your breath is shallow your brains (mainly the cerebrum) doesn't get the proper amounts of energy (air). The cerebrum has a right hemisphere and a left hemisphere that make up the whole. The law of the opposites says that you must have a balance to function properly. Most people with western philosophy US, Canada, Europe, England, and France all think mostly with the left hemisphere. While the eastern peoples think more with their right hemisphere. The difference can be seen in the chart:

THE RIGHT HEMISPHERE	THE LEFT HEMISPHERE
Unify, spiritual, harmony	Separates, material, disharmony
Comprehends the whole sentences and acts of Extracting the significance from a series of related units	Comprehends each letter an acts of speaking And verbal thinking are a process that occurs in a series of steps one at a time
Unification and Integration	Segregation and Differentiation
Sees similarities between things	Separates whole into parts/ Whole presented a part at a time

Synthetically, Holistic, Congregative	Analytical, Linear, Deductive
Introverted	*Extroverted*
Focuses on the inner culture	*Focuses on the outer culture*

As you can see, constantly being extroverted in consciousness (focus on the environment) makes you use your left hemisphere of the brain, much more than your right hemisphere. This causes you to be in an illusionary type of setting, do to the fact that the left hemisphere deals with outside of the body, focusing on material and separating yourself from others. Thinking that we are not one big human family but separate from the whole. You are more likely to use discrimination and segregation to their extremes. They always want more material possessions like money, cars, or just power over others since you feel separated from the whole. These hemispheric differences are not randomly distributed through society. Men in general are more left-sided thinking than women and so are members of the pale race, in comparison to people with massive amounts of melanin. This is why women use the right hemisphere of harmony and can get along better as a whole better than men and why blacks (right sided) and pale people (left sided) think and act differently. This hemispheric difference is a well-known fact to western psychologists. **You will learn that hemispheric differences and historical events, (of different races on earth) are different, do to this fact, that without this concept of the different hemisphere's there can be no science or history, or psychology, or anthropology, or even that of religion.**

Psychology (Thought process) of Blacks and Whites
Blacks--Whites

Right Hemisphere and Mid Brian thought that's characterized by spiritual concepts - love- sharing- affection Midbrain- balances rational thought with creative thought	Left Hemisphere thought that's characterized by Egotism-individualism It also intellectualizes and rationalizes
Thought concepts of words based on story in which words are use (emotional content) Ex. Bad can mean - good, moderate, or excellence	Thoughts linear - Words have fixed meaning – no slang we put it
Family Centered	Self Centered
Individual valued based on individual contributions- You are what you do.	Individual valued based what you own You are what you own.
Things are Society Owned	Things are Privately Owned

African Science------------------------------European Science

All things are controlled by seen and unseen forces	They use the word accident and coincidence or it's caused by seen forces
Human is make up of three parts- Mind, Body, Spirit- at same time	No two things can occupy the same space at the same time
Earth has its own heat -- ex. Dead body can not hold internal heat	Sun gives earth heat

Our-story (history from the black man perspective) records that evil arising from the unbalanced expression of the left hemisphere far exceeds in destructfulness, those of right hemisphere people. All races had slavery but African slavery was not the same kind of

Michael Campbell

slavery then pale peoples. African slavery was temporary and you kind of joined the family of the slaveholder. The slave was set free if he or she joined the religion of the slaveholder because they knew that we all one family in the end. The pale slavery was heinous and wicked for it kept slaves as servants and treated them like animals because they thought that they were separate from themselves (extreme left sided thinking). African's did not separate the slaves' family either but the pale people did and went as far as to kill the pregnant mother of male slaves to put fear in their children. The left hemisphere is primarily for man's inhumanity and cruelty to man and most of the social disharmony. Even though it carries a big price it is also responsible for technology (by wanting to control everything) and the satisfaction of pleasures (satisfy emotions). The right hemisphere is responsible for the stagnation in physical technology but science and religion are intrinsic products of the right hemisphere cultures are now being used by the left sided cultures. The left hemisphere cultures are totally incapable with the true religious, scientific, and spiritual thinking. This is why before 1 AD the western culture contributed nothing to civilization and still indebted to the black nation for their foundations of scientific and religious thought. The reason pale people like rare meat most of the time is because while in Europe before they came to America they new very little on how to cultivate the land to grow vegetables. They ate mostly meats and all kinds of it because they had no agriculture till the Indians and the black slaves showed them how to farm. This is why blacks were in the field most of the time, and not in the mines, because only the black nations knew (for thousands of years) how to cultivate the lands. This is also why the scientific and religious validation of false doctrines, practices, and institutions are now controlling the nations and dominating the world setting trends for other countries.

It is the spiritual side or the right hemisphere of the brain that is introverted (focuses on the inside) in consciousness that leads to Knowledge of Self. What makes people with color different is melanin. Melanin being a transducer for intangible signals (energies) automatically puts us in touch with right hemisphere of the brain. That's why pales and blacks see things

so differently cause they are working on two totally different thinking modes. *When melanin becomes toxic due to over eating, lack of vitamin B, drugs or just bad living it makes black people act primitive and they become hateful and violent.* <u>*The education system in school fails to reach some of our black children because they are naturally thinking uses the right-side of the Brian and school is mainly taught to the left side, of the brain thinking culture*</u>*. Since pale people are more naturally left side than black kids they go through school a little easier then blacks since schools were designed for them. The Intelligence Quotient (IQ) Testing is one of the greatest hoaxes perpetrated on humankind for the purpose of racial, class exploitation, and discrimination. The western concept of intelligence and its development in the educational environment were there must be a clear distinction between made memorizing and understanding. A student must overstand not just memorize. Depth of knowledge isn't just knowing details and the IQ test is devised in such a manner that thirty percent of the questions depend on culture, personal and parental education. While the IQ testing barely even measures the left hemisphere of the brain, for it really measures people's degree of cultural and educational knowledge. It is a clever way of "certifying" certain sectors of the population "more competent" than others for best educational, and employment opportunities. How can one be a leader of a country who's not morally cultivated to know right from wrong and this is why there is so much crime in your government because you got thieves running the country. In court the judge doesn't judge any big cases, the jurors do, so why call him a judge then. The judge is a supervisor between the two opposing parties. They only judge over low penalty cases but in big ones, the jurors judge, (who have not been cultivated either) so the blind judges the blind (thence phrase - justice is blind). The reason why technology is getting out of control is because the left-sided thinkers are always trying to make things easier and better. That's why people they are getting fat and lazy because technology makes it easy for them to do nothing productive. This is also why the rivers and oceans are polluted, the air is polluted, and forests are being destroyed. All this for technology, with no regard for nature or the planet earth is wrong. Since the left-sided thinkers think only of themselves and*

Michael Campbell

not for the things around them, it is easier for them not to give it the respect it is due. Black, brown, red, yellow, and pale people need a balance and only very few are cultivating themselves to get it. In this application I have given you the process of achieving cultivation from man to god body to use and insperience the true reality of things. <u>I have showed that consciousness and thought are connected by how you think</u>. If you're always thinking in a material and limited way rather than thinking immaterial and unlimited (spiritual) you won't form transducers to understand it because our thought patterns won't allow immaterial or spiritual thoughts to be accessed. Shallow breathing causes one to have an imbalance in the energies of the cerebrum's hemispheres, which is lack of energy in the mind that leads to low consciousness. Left side of the brain thinking people mostly see what's on the outside of themselves in their deductive, linear, and analytical thinking leads them to think they know something because they have a definition for it (memorizing not knowing). <u>Being informed or having information is not the same thing as knowing, for knowing is experienced or insperienced in self</u>. Knowing is a feeling that is directly related to Self. Reception of information, names, definitions, and descriptions are trying to make up for the knowledge of reality itself. This is why jobs don't want college graduates without experience in their field because having the information about something is not true knowing. The false definitions we give to emotions and their various forms is why so many people fall under their influence. <u>Emotional manifestation involves the induction of tension in some part of the body, in most cases it involves lifting of the chest which render breathing shallow and throws off the rhythm of breathe to hyperventilation</u>. Hyperventilation causes a state of a trance that is a distortion in thinking and perception. This why people act so crazy when put in tense situations. The same type of effect is felt with stress and stressful situations. In situation when you become stressed you call it an emotion like frustration, angry, disappointment, or sad. These definitions mean nothing without the experience or insperience (inside Self) that gives the definitions of emotions they're meaning. This is even subject to change because each person insperiences emotions in different degrees.

OVERSTANDING DARKNESS

Behavioral professionals teach people how to be successful in their life by emphasizing the need and importance of identifying ourselves with thoughts that are unlimited in our abilities to achieve goals. One must keep in mind that humans ability to know, to do, and to be are essentially unlimited. Don't limit yourself in any way because you are only clouding your judgment on what you think you can achieve. The major source of problems in people's lives is their ignorance of the suggestive power of beliefs. Believe you can do something and it will probably come true but the same thing is true if you believe that you can't, you probably won't. The major obstruction to your ability to know the truth is the delusion of determining what is valid from the fact that the majority holds a certain belief to be true. The truth cannot be established by consensus, since most people believe in definition of reality as the truth, instead of experience or insperiencing reality for themselves. *If one believes a definition to be true, than you believe in someone's opinion to be true, not the reality of the truth itself. Godlike powers dwell within your spirit but cannot be raised to the foreground (top) and guide the external apexes of your life without the total devotion to its resurrection. Use this doctrine in a serious and devoted way so that the Higher Self within your spirit will rise and Light your mind with righteousness. Being loving and charitable are ways to allow the Divine Self to take control and give you happiness never thought of before. When you do wrong against others by being selfish and hateful, this action keeps the indwelling divinity from resurrecting. You are liable for your failure to develop the proper use of your higher faculties and spiritually cultivating yourself to a higher level of consciousness.* **Humans cannot develop into a divine being if she or he isn't compelled to live in truth.** *Freedom to choose in all situations doesn't mean we have the right to violate the Creator's Universal Laws. We violate the laws by giving into fear caused by the absence of the material means of dealing with obstruction and injustices of others. Nothing can stand up against the Creator's Power in the defense of the just and what is right. The purpose for being on this earth is the resurrection of this indwelling intelligence so it can guide our endeavors (efforts) in life with the same omniscience that it uses to guide physiological*

Michael Campbell

and subconscious mental activities. For this creative genius of the divine intelligence inside self to rise, then you must die to things of this world and place yourself beyond the control of earthly things to awaken the spiritual power to accomplish all things.

PART V THE CONSCIOUSNESS AND THE SUBCONSCIOUS

A.   CONSCIOUSNESS
B.   SUBCONSCIOUS

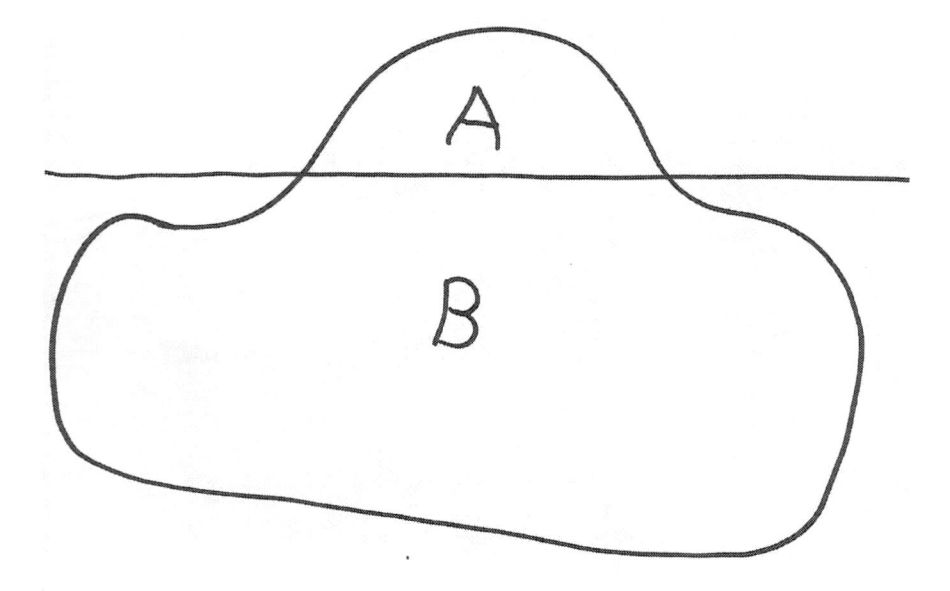

A.   Consciousness- the will, potential to act, to do
B.   Subconscious- the power to act and to do

The first thing that you notice from this picture of the conscious and subconscious is that the subconscious carries the majority of the work to be done. The subconscious lacks the ability on how it's programmed and education limits itself to influencing the conscious part of being. The subconscious is programmed by the conscious mind, by the thoughts you think, and the things you do and like. The subconscious cannot distinguish between reality and your imagination. This is why meditation it is so important in changing behavior to see yourself in your imagination doing the opposite of the unwanted behavior. This is the biggest problem with people who want to change their behavior because they don't know how the process works. One needs unity between the conscious and the subconscious parts of your being to fulfill goals and change any behavior. All unwanted behaviors like drugs use, intense emotional influence, and all the undesirable things that happen are a result of the action taken by subconscious. These actions are programmed by our consciousness, Willed or Unwilled, over the course of our lives. To truly achieve personal and social harmony and prosperity in the lives of people, it requires the unlearning of undesirable behaviors, and replacing them with their opposites. <u>*When you struggle with right and wrong you are struggling against the energies that are experienced as desires and emotions. These energies are separate from the part of being that's beyond the emotions and desires and not under there influence.*</u>

The Individual- is the joining of the "indivisible" and "duality". Humans are composed of two entities.

1. **Higher half being "SELF " Divine Nature - A** *piece of God Consciousness (Supreme view)*
2. **Lower half being "PERSON" Animal Nature -** *A piece of animal consciousness (personal view)*

LOWER HALF- PERSON	HIGHER HALF- SELF
Makes your personality	*Not influenced by pleasure or displeasure*
Emotional patterns	*No emotional patterns*
Is subject to change	*Is always influences the same way, never changes*

If you concentrate on yourself for a moment you will see that throughout your life there's a part of you that was always the same. It always try's to guide you to do the right thing almost like your conscience but it observes your action and the reason for them. This is Self. You will also notice that there is a part of you that always changed as your knowledge, wisdom, and overstanding grew. The things you used to like, now that you know better, you don't do them anymore. This part of you is your person or Ego that controls most of the people in the world and gives rise to fulfilling desires and passions that lead to crimes and violence. Your awareness of this difference depends on your degree of detached introspection. In other words if you can step outside your low self (detach from the Ego) you can see your thoughts and emotions for what they really are. A major source of problems in most behavior shaping systems in the world, in religion, in psychology, etc, are designed for the lower part of man's being (the person or animal nature) as this identity. This lower part is subjected to finding pleasure in things that are injuriously evil, just to please ones desires or passions. This is because there is nothing in its nature that has the ability to discriminate between right and wrong, good and evil. This is why they fail in religions because they appeal to the lower nature that is controlled by emotions and desires. Only by developing and strengthening the expression of your higher part of being (Self) in the day-to-day activity of an individual will change occur. Since the subconscious has no distinction between reality and imagination, believe it and it will come true. The power of belief, by concentrating hard or mediating throughout the day, on higher topics of the spirit and the pursuit of knowledge, will cause change since you are what you think. Make self-evaluation in your life to overstand what Knowledge of Self is about. By mere striving means that the majority of people lives are characterized by the non-identification with the Higher Self and they identify with the lower nature with its addiction to sensual and emotional pleasures. Some people feel the higher natures presence but identify with the lower nature, they get confused that the emotional and pleasurable motivated behavior is not apart of their True Self.

PART IV THE UNIVERSAL LAWS
1. Law of Attitude

It's the principle that every experience in life is controlled by your attitude towards it. If you stump your toe you can focus on the pain until it disables you. On the other hand, if you take it as a spirit's message to be careful and say ouch, then go on about your business.

2. *Law of Karma*
It's the highest form of justice that we create for ourselves in payment of past deeds; both good and bad. Karma is the system that returns to each of us, without favoritism, every act ever performed along our evolutionary path, and returns those acts in like kind. If you are abusive, you'll be abused. Every time you say "Treat others as you would have them treat you," "Love thy neighbor as thy self," "What you sow, you shall reap," and many other you're reciting the Law of Karma.

3. *Law of Avoidance*
To refuse to handle a tough situation or to deny your full potential or to neglect doing something that should be done will effect the physical body, the mental health, emotional stability and even affairs in your life. That situation will follow you through each incarnation, until the correct action is taken to balance that, which has been avoided.

4. *Law of Activity*
Every thought creates an alchemical process in the conscious mind. <u>Every action has three elements:</u>

    A. The thought which conceived it
    B. The will which finds a way to perform the thought
    C. The action which is the combination of the thought and the will

Therefore an action is a direct result of the strength of the thought and the power of the will or the will being controlled by emotions. Nothing therefore happens by accident. We cannot deny *responsibility for our action.*

5. *Law of Continuity*
Nothing in the universe ever dies, is lost, or is destroyed. Everything simply changes form, and becomes a part of forever.

6. ***Law of Consequence***

Each of us has pure free will, whether we choose to exercise it or not. In the failure to exercise our free will, we are yielding that gift to an outside force to make our choices for us. We have the free will to control all things in our life, at all times. However we must be aware that we will suffer the consequences of each choice and decision, whether made by us or by another. The responsibility for the use of free will is ours and we are charged with taking responsibility for our decisions and our actions.

Notice that everything in life depends on you to do the right things. It is your attitude, actions, and activity that make your life hard and miserable or easy and good. These laws aren't to be broken without some price to pay. These laws are in full effect all over the universe to all of the Creator's beings and spiritual entities.

Relationships with others and Self

Always remember that all throughout your life you have been involved in relationships, with people you don't know but see occasionally, with friends and family, to your environment, and the most important relationship is the one with yourself. If you cannot have a fruitful relationship with yourself, than you cannot have a fruitful relationship with anyone else. Most of your relationships with other people and things go un-noticed, not to mention the relationship with Self. First improve your Self-relationship and all others will fall in line. You will start to overstand all the many relationships you have with anything and everything you come in contact with. This is why personal relationships fail mainly because you have failed at or not even recognized all the relationship you are in (like the one with this writing your reading now). Everything in life must start with self for life to make any kind of sense at all.

You must overstand that the Creator dwells within you, so studying Self is like theology, only when you know who you are and where you have been can you know without a shadow of a doubt where you are going.

Books for Overstanding

1) The Akasha Records - 1000
2) The Enuma Elish - 7
3) The Atra-Hasis - 3
4) The Tablet of Anuz -3
5) Nergal and Arishkegal - 1

Twelve minor great teacher's: Chapters
Hosea - 14 Joel - 3
Amos – 9 Obadiah - 1
Jonah – 4 Micah - 7

6) Tammuz an Ishtar - 1
7) The Descent of Ishtar - 1
8) The Tablet of Etana - 3
9) The Tablet of Adapa - 1
10) The Gilgamesh Epics - 12

Nahum – 3 Zephaniah - 3
Habbakuk – 3 Haggai – 2
Zechariah – 14 Malachi - 4

77) The pages of Zakar, Adam ten, Nekaybaw prophetess during Zakar's time. "The Tablets of sin" Seth, fifty, "The Tablets of Time," Adafa, Enoch, and "The Tablets of Generations" Abraham, ten, total one hundred pages and the nineteen Scrolls of Wisdom:

At Tawraat, The Law.

*Genesis – 50   Exdos - 40
Leviticus – 27   Numbers -36
Deuteronomy - 34
Ketubim: The Holy Writing
The Psalms – 150   Proverbs - 31
Job – 42   Song of Solomon - 8
Ruth – 4   Lamnentations - 5
Ecclesiates – 12   Esther - 10
Daniel – 12   Ezra - 10
Nehemiah 13   1st Chronicles - 29
2nd Chronicles – 36 Total 13
The New Testament
Matthew – 28   Mark - 16
Luke – 24   John - 21
James – 5   Judah – 1 Total 6
The Letters of John, Just letters to a Girlfriend; Not Holy Scriptures
1st John – 5   2nd John – 1
3rd John – 1*

Neb'im: The Scrolls of the Prophets

*Joshua – 24   Judges - 21
1st Samuel – 31   2nd Samuel – 24
1st Kings – 22   2nd Kings - 25
Isaiah – 66   Jeremiah - 52
Ezekiel – 48   Hosea - 14
Joel – 3   Amos – 9
Obadiah – 1   Jonah - 4
Micah – 7   Nahum - 3
Habbukuk – 3   Zephaniah - 3
Malachi – 4   Total 20
Faker Books of the Black Devil trying to mislead tashua's True Followers: Romans - 16
1st Corinthians – 16   2nd Corinthians - 13
Galatians – 6   Ephesians - 6
Philippians – 4   Colossians – 4   1stThessalonians - 5/ 2ndThessalonians - 3*

*1st John – 5   2nd John – 1
3rd John 1   Total 7
Philemon – 1   Hebrews – 13
1st Peter – 5   2nd Peter – 3
1st Timothy – 4   Titus - 3 Total 17*

Apocrypha: The Hidden Books of the Bible
1) The Third Book of Esdras
2) The Fourth Book of Esdras
3) The Book of Tobit
4) The Book of Judith
5) The Book of Esther
6) The Book of Wisdom (Solomon)
7) The Wisdom of Jesus the son of Sirach
8) & 9) The Book of Baruch
10,11,12) The addition to Daniels
13) The Prayer of Manasses
14) **The 1ˢᵗ Book of the Maccabees**
15) **The 2ⁿᵈ Book of the Maccabees**
16) The 3ʳᵈ Book of the Maccabees
17) The 4ᵗʰ Book of the Maccabees

18) Among the other Apocryphal writing are the Old Testament maybe enumerated:
1) The Book of Iubilees, or the Little Genesis
2) **The Book of Enoch**
3) The Assumptions of Moses
4) The Ascension of Isaiah
5) The Apocalypse of Baruch
6) The Sibylline Oracles
7) The Psalter of Solomon
8) **The Urantia Book 4**
9) The Testament of the Twelve Patriarchs

From the Holy Tablets-Chapter Six-The Human Breast-tablet 8:68-8:78

Add to these the Torah, Koran, Egyptian Book of the Dead, Buddhism, Zen, The Holy Tablet, The Metu Neter volumes one & two-the Egyptian System of Spiritual Cultivation, Breathe Control, Meditation, Aura's, Charkas, Body of light, The Book of the 5%, Code of the Samurai, Hemp!-the Billion Dollar Crop, Dead Sea Scroll, The Bio-Mind Experiment, Intuition, Empathy, nutrition and healing,

Celestial Fire, the Zodiac, Yoga philosophy, The Tree of Knowledge, The Ankh, Enoch's 64 Keys, The Tree of Life, The Urantia book and knowledge of Self that show me my connection with the Creator. On a smaller scale we humans have infinite ability to know, to be, and to learn. We are unconditioned at the core, we have no likes or dislikes just patterns of individual consciousness. The more moral fiber, the more impact is felt in just living. As Mental Principles give way to revelations our spirits are enhance as conscious effort used to live morally. It is like living by an internal code of justice, far more complicated then man's laws. I have written this book to give you ways of elevating your consciousness. ONLY THROUGH CONSCIOUS EFFORT CAN ANY PROGRESS BE MADE.

About the Author

I was born in Rochester, New York the middle child of three boys. I went to the Army Reserves at an early age, just 17 years old, still in high school. I went to basic training over my 11th grade summer in high school and three days after I graduate I went Regular Army. Wanting a little college money from school and ended up fighting in a war (Just Cause). I got out at the age of 21 where I went to a community college and received an Associates Degree in Social Science. I worked for Xerox for 5 years before getting laid off. I went back to school to get my bachelor Degree in Psychology from Brockport University. While working at Xerox I got a chance to study many scriptures of the Bibles and other sources and I wanted to share some with you: This table is from the Holy Tablets;

Made in the USA
Lexington, KY
20 August 2014